The Pursuit of Development

Previous Books by Ian Goldin

Age of Discovery: Navigating the Risks and Rewards of Our New Renaissance

The Butterfly Defect: How Globalization Creates Systemic Risks, and What to Do about It

Is the Planet Full?

Divided Nations: Why Global Governance Is Failing, and What We Can Do about It

Exceptional People: How Migration Shaped our World and Will Define our Future

Globalization for Development: Meeting New Challenges

The Case for Aid

The Economics of Sustainable Development

Economic Reform, Trade and Agricultural Development

Modelling Economy-wide Reforms

Trade Liberalization: Global Economic Implications

Open Economies

The Future of Agriculture

Economic Crisis: Lessons from Brazil

Making Race: The Economics and Politics of Identity

PRAISE FOR *THE PURSUIT OF DEVELOPMENT*

'Ian Goldin has been in the engine room of policy and action in South Africa, a leading figure in the World Bank and at the head of one of the world's most important research institutions in Oxford. This important book reflects the richness of his experience and scholarship. It shows how development can be fostered as well as the vulnerabilities, complexities and risks. It is succinct, wise, well-informed, broad ranging and deep. It is also very accessible and admirable in its brevity. A splendid achievement.'

Lord Nicholas Stern, President of the British Academy, and IG Patel Professor of Economics and Government, London School of Economics.

'I strongly recommend Ian Goldin's excellent book—a 'must read' for anyone interested in development. He shows why some people and some countries stay poor while others get rich. This highly accessible book identifies what development means, why it matters and what we can all do to improve our world.'

Sir Suma Chakrabarti, President of the European Bank for Reconstruction and Development and former Permanent Secretary of the United Kingdom Department of International Development and of the Ministry of Justice.

'*The Pursuit of Development* by Ian Goldin could not have come at a better time. The adoption of Sustainable Development Goals puts a high premium on our understanding of how development happens at a time when the global economic landscape is undergoing seismic changes. The rigour of analysis and the broad approach to the evolution of thinking beyond the narrow economic approach over time is one which will greatly benefit the younger generation students of development. I highly recommend this primer.'

Donald Kaberuka, President of the African Development Bank (2005 to 2015) and formerly Minister of Finance, Rwanda.

'Every citizen should be a champion of, and contributor to, sustainable development. Ian Goldin's book is a great starting point for understanding our current sustainable development challenges and future possibilities, including the end of poverty in our time. The book offers a succinct, highly readable, and reasoned introduction to the debates and the data, from the vantage point of a world-leading development thinker and practitioner.'

Jeffrey D. Sachs, Special Advisor to the UN Secretary-General on the Sustainable Development Goals and author of *The Age of Sustainable Development*.

'Anyone interested in development should read *The Pursuit of Development*. Development remains the greatest challenge for humanity. Drawing on his remarkable experience, Ian Goldin looks both back and forward to address the remaining old and the many emerging challenges, including rising inequality and climate change. I strongly recommend this immensely readable, timely and vitally important book.'

Kumi Naidoo, International Executive Director, Greenpeace and former Secretary General, Civicus.

'Ian Goldin looks at the complexities of development in our interconnected world, and does what so few do. Joining up the dots, he looks beyond the narrowly economic, and beyond Governments to people. He considers the important role played by social movements and by those in a broad range of organisations. He tells us that we all have a part to play if only we continue learning. A must read.'

Baroness Valerie Amos, Former UN Under-Secretary-General for Humanitarian and Emergency Relief, Director of SOAS, University of London.

The Pursuit of Development

Economic Growth, Social Change, and Ideas

IAN GOLDIN

OXFORD
UNIVERSITY PRESS

OXFORD

UNIVERSITY PRESS

Great Clarendon Street, Oxford, OX2 6DP,
United Kingdom

Oxford University Press is a department of the University of Oxford.
It furthers the University's objective of excellence in research, scholarship,
and education by publishing worldwide. Oxford is a registered trade mark of
Oxford University Press in the UK and in certain other countries

First Edition published in 2016

Impression: 1

Published in the United States of America by Oxford University Press
198 Madison Avenue, New York, NY 10016, United States of America

British Library Cataloguing in Publication Data
Data available

Library of Congress Control Number: 2015956178

ISBN 978-0-19-877803-5

Printed in Great Britain by
Clays Ltd, St Ives plc

To the memory of my mother
Who taught me to look and learn

CONTENTS

PREFACE AND ACKNOWLEDGEMENTS

How individuals and societies develop over time is a key question for global citizens. Development motivates and intrigues me. I have worked in and with developing countries for my entire career and it has been a privilege to be asked by Oxford University Press to distil my experience into this short volume.

I have trained and worked as an economist and so my perspective is largely informed by the economic literature and my engagement in economic policy. As a Vice President and the Director of Development Policy for the World Bank Group, Head of Programmes at the Organisation for Economic Co-operation and Development (OECD) Development Centre, and principal economist at the European Bank of Reconstruction and Development (EBRD), as well as in my role as Chief Executive of the Development Bank of Southern Africa (DBSA) and advisor to President Mandela, and more recently as the Senior Independent Director of the United Kingdom Government's aid agency CDC, I have drawn on the wisdom of numerous scholars, policymakers, and members of the development community. Principal among them has been Nick Stern, who has informed my understanding of the role of ideas. Having represented both developing country and global institutions at different stages of my career I have learnt that the position one sits in necessarily informs one's views. In practice however, every circumstance is different and there is no theory or lesson that may be replicated everywhere.

In my current role as Director of the interdisciplinary Oxford Martin School and Professor of Globalisation and Development at the University of Oxford, I have come to appreciate the pitfalls of narrow economic perspectives. All our futures will be shaped by trends which transcend national borders, as they do academic disciplinary silos. Demographic, climate, health, technological, and other developments will shape all our destinies. The future of developing countries is intertwined with those of the most advanced economies. Widening our perspectives beyond our narrow professional and national perspectives is more vital than ever.

If there is one thing this book shows it is that there is the need for constant learning. The evolution in our understanding of development makes me optimistic. We have come a long way. But there is much we still do not understand and much more to learn.

A short book is necessarily selective. All of the topics I have covered are the subject of fuller analysis elsewhere, and parts of this volume draw on my previous books. I am most grateful to my co-authors for their insights and to the many colleagues, scholars, and policymakers from whom I have been most fortunate to learn over the past decades.

This volume owes much to the remarkable depth and breadth of David Clark's knowledge of development. David helped me shape the proposal for this book and has subsequently played a vital role in identifying key texts and helping lay the foundations for the book, as well as preparing its figures and tables, and contributing to my response to the referees' reports and polishing the final text. Maximilia Lane provided excellent research assistance in the drafting of Chapter 1. John Edwards, a recent graduate in development at Oxford, went through the early draft, improving the flow and identifying shortcomings in my coverage, and Sarah Cliffe has generously provided very timely and helpful advice on my understanding of conflict and development. My son Alex offered candid and constructive comments and daughter Olivia drew on her English and Development Economics studies to improve the entire final text.

OUP has once again proved to be a remarkable publishing partner. Andrea Keegan encouraged me to write this book and Jenny Nugee has provided timely expert guidance throughout the publication process, supported by her many tremendously helpful Oxford colleagues and Saraswathi Ethiraju and others in India. I also am grateful to two anonymous reviewers and have sought to incorporate their helpful comments.

My purpose in writing the book is to convey my passion and interest in development and the progress being made through the combination of learning and doing. Development is a team sport that requires the engagement of civil servants, businessmen and women, scholars, non-government organizations, and citizens in all countries.

I hope that this volume increases your interest and your ability to contribute to the success of global development.

Ian Goldin

Oxford, February 2016

LIST OF FIGURES

LIST OF TABLES

1

------ ∞∞∞ ------

What is Development?

Too many people in the world still live in desperate poverty. About 900 million people live on less than $1.90 a day, the World Bank's definition of extreme poverty. Over a billion people live on less than two dollars a day and are deprived of the means to lead a decent life. Why is this so? And what can be done? These are amongst the most important questions facing humanity at the start of the new millennium.

Progress in tackling poverty over the past twenty-five years has been remarkable. The Millennium Development Goal primary target, to cut the 1990 poverty rate in half, was achieved in 2010. For the first time in history, there is the real possibility of eliminating extreme poverty in our life-times. To achieve this, we need to understand how development happens.

A hundred years ago, Argentina was amongst the seven wealthiest nations in the world, but now ranks 56th in terms of its per capita income. In 1950, Ghana's per capita income was higher than that of South Korea; now South Korean people are more than eleven times wealthier than the citizens of Ghana. Meanwhile, whilst in recent decades over 3 billion people have seen remarkable improvements in health, education, and incomes, more than twenty *failed states* and over a billion people have seen little progress in development.

Within countries, the contrast is even greater than between countries. Extraordinary achievements enjoyed by some occur alongside both the absolute and relative deprivation of others. What is true for advanced societies, such as the United Kingdom and United States, is even more so in most, but not all, developing countries.

Some countries have grown rapidly, but have lagged behind others in terms of social achievements. Equatorial Guinea has grown even faster than China since the discovery of oil in 1996. Average per capita income expanded from $1,970 in 2000 to $17,430 in 2014. Yet few people have shared in this new-found prosperity. Despite now having a per capita income similar to Estonia or the Czech Republic (and higher than almost all other African countries), life expectancy has barely improved since the turn of the century and has averaged under fifty years. Meanwhile, considerably poorer African countries such as Ethiopia have managed to increase life expectancy by sixteen years since 1990.

In other cases, low or modest growth has been associated with sustained improvements in social indicators. Bangladesh has made steady progress with literacy and life expectancy over the last twenty-five years, even though per capita income remains low (around $1,093). In India the state of Kerala (which is home to over 33 million people), has persistently outperformed other Indian states in virtually all social indicators including literacy, life expectancy, infant mortality, under-nourishment, and fertility. Yet several Indian states enjoy higher per capita incomes.

This book seeks to explain the pursuit of development through eight thematic chapters, each of which draws on development theory and practice and an interdisciplinary perspective.

The Meaning of 'Development'

There are many definitions of development and the concept itself has evolved rapidly over recent decades. To develop is to grow, which many economists and policymakers have taken to mean economic growth. Yet development is not confined to economic growth. Development is no longer the preserve of economists and the subject itself has enjoyed rapid evolution to become the object of interdisciplinary scholarship drawing on politics, sociology, psychology, history, geography, anthropology, medicine, and many other disciplines.

While Development Studies is relatively new as an academic discipline, the questions being asked are not—philosophers have puzzled over them for millennia. Our questions are rooted in both classical political economy and ancient philosophy, such as Aristotle's notions of well-being and human flourishing. Many of the giants of classical economics were also concerned with this intersection of economic and philosophical thought. Adam Smith worried about the 'progress of opulence' and the necessities of achieving self-respect; he recognized the importance of being able to appear in public unashamed and argued that people need certain basic necessities, such as linen shirts or leather shoes, to avoid shame, depending on custom and social convention.

In this volume, our focus is on the economic and social development of societies and people's lives. Leading scholars have long recognized that economic development cannot be equated with economic growth. For Paul Streeten development aims 'to provide all human beings with the opportunity for a full life', while for Dudley Seers it should create 'the conditions for the realization of human personality'. Such concerns have been more fully articulated by Amartya Sen's Capability Approach, which views development in terms of capabilities or substantive 'freedoms' people have reason to value.

Why are Some Countries Rich and Others Poor?

Until the 1980s development policy mainly focused on generating economic growth. In purely economic terms, growth increases when *total factor productivity*, or the efficiency of production, increases. An increase in a country's use of labour and capital, or its greater efficiency, provides for economic growth. Growth can be associated with increases in investment in resources, including education and health, leading to *capital accumulation*, or an increase in wealth. It also can result from changes in the way these resources are used, leading to *structural transformation* of economies, in which there is a reallocation of economic activity, typically from agriculture to manufacturing and services.

While development cannot be reduced to economic growth only, economic growth is often necessary to facilitate development. Growth is generally needed to eradicate poverty, because in poor societies without economic growth there are insufficient resources to invest in education, health, infrastructure, and the other foundations of development. Because economic growth is an important engine of development, the measurement of development for many years was often reduced to economic indicators only. However, growth alone is insufficient, as is evident from the continued prevalence of dire poverty in many countries which have enjoyed sustained growth.

Development is necessarily in part a normative or value-based concept. What would make me feel better off is not necessarily the same as what would make you feel better off and the balance between different dimensions of development requires subjective judgements. Nevertheless, development thinkers and policymakers try to find measureable features of life to set goals of development and judge success and failure according to thresholds. Numerous measurements and assumptions are employed to derive such common frameworks, which draw on both objective criteria and subjective judgements. The World Bank's poverty threshold of $1.90 a day embodies wide-ranging assumptions, as does the categorization of 'low', 'middle', and 'advanced' economies. Similarly, there is a ceiling of $1,215 for the per capita national income levels that in 2015 qualified seventy-seven countries to be defined as 'low income', and therefore eligible for highly concessional lending from the World Bank and other multilateral banks. The World Bank's recent revision of the poverty threshold to $1.90 per day, whereas previously it had been $1.25, transformed overnight the number of people defined as poor and their global distribution. This is indicative of the somewhat arbitrary nature of the measurement of poverty. Similarly significant assumptions also are embedded in the comparison across countries, using wildly fluctuating exchange rates and their adjustments to purchasing power parity (PPP).

The most common measure of economic growth is Gross Domestic Product (GDP) which measures a country's national output and expenditure. Gross National Product (GNP) measures the products and services produced by all citizens of a given country, adding the balance between income flowing in from abroad and outflows from the country. If the outflow of income to foreign assets is greater than the inflow of income from abroad, GNP will be smaller than GDP. Gross National Income (GNI) measures the domestic and foreign output of all residents of a country.

GDP is the most widely used measure of development as it is relatively easy to calculate, accessible, quantifiable, and comparable across borders. Dividing GDP by the population gives GDP per capita, which is a widely used benchmark as it reflects levels of average development by accounting for discrepancies in population size. To overcome the distortions that arise when comparing incomes or expenditures across countries using nominal (official) exchange rates, the concept of purchasing power parities (PPP) was introduced, as early as 1940. PPP aims to compare a country's product against its international price, so that economists can see how much a bundle of comparable products and services will cost a consumer in different countries and hence compare absolute and relative wealth internationally.

These widely used measures are only partial indicators of development and have many shortcomings. For instance, these summary economic measures give an indication of a country's market production and are not an indication of economic well-being or quality of life, as they leave out factors such as education, health, and life expectancy. With similar levels of average per capita incomes, average life expectancy is Bangladesh is seventy-one years, while it is fifty-seven in Zimbabwe and sixty-two in Tanzania.

Furthermore, per capita measures tend to obscure distributional dimensions of development and two countries with the same per capita levels may face very different development challenges. Averages may hide wide-ranging disparities between rich and poor. For example, while the United States and Denmark share similar GDPs per capita, in the United States the richest one per cent of the population earns over 20 per cent of the income, which is more than the bottom 90 per cent of the population. By contrast, in Denmark, the top one per cent of the population earns seven per cent of national income.

Another shortcoming of the summary economic measures is that certain 'intermediary' products, or products whose sole purpose is to allow or facilitate the creation or sale of 'final' products, are not traded and not captured by GDP; and neither are many services. For example, household-supplied healthcare, education, transport, cooking, childcare, and other non-traded goods do not appear in

GDP calculations. As many of these services are supplied by women, the contributions of women to economic activity, as well as the actual levels of overall economic activity, are underestimated.

A further problem is that activities which are unfavourable for development can provide positive boosts to economic indicators. For example, an increase in violence and crime that increases the demand for medical and security services could raise national output and GDP. So too can the extraction of non-renewable resources and utilization of products that cause pollution (such as coal or other fossil fuels). Resource depletion, such as the extraction of water from non-renewable aquifers, as well as externalities and spillover effects, such as climate change and pollution, are largely ignored in the output-based measurement of national accounts.

By the 1970s, twenty-five years of post-war development suggested an uneven track record. A number of remarkable success stories, not least in East Asia (giving rise to a series of books and critiques of the so-called 'East Asian Miracle') highlighted the extent to which development could happen, sometimes very rapidly. But in Latin America and Africa, rapid growth had not necessarily lowered poverty. Some economists argued that the benefits of economic growth would trickle down and even that inequality was necessary for growth, at least temporarily. By the 1970s, the recognition that economic growth alone need not translate into improved well-being led to a broadening of approaches to development.

Beyond Growth

Economic growth was not necessarily a tide that lifted all people. Feeding on unequal income and asset distribution, growth can concentrate wealth further, making the rich richer and leaving the poor behind. By the 1970s, it had become apparent that while many economies had experienced economic growth, many of the poorest countries had grown more slowly, and, within most developing countries, the poorest individuals had not benefited sufficiently to escape poverty.

The development economist Dudley Seers argued that to address poverty broader measurement was needed. Since GNP can grow considerably without resulting in a reduction in poverty, unemployment, or inequality, he called for 'the dethronement of GNP' as the primary measure of development. While recognizing that economic growth was needed to help increase the incomes of the poor, Seers argued that development requires a decline in poverty, unemployment, and inequality.

Hollis Chenery, Richard Jolly, and Montek Ahluwalia, amongst others, argued for *redistribution with growth*. In their view, policymakers did not have to make a compromise between growth and reducing poverty and inequality. Instead, distributional objectives should form part of any development policy plan. They argued for the need to maximize GNP growth, and redistribute investment and income to increase welfare for the poor. The incomes of the wealthy would be taxed to fund public services that would increase the productivity of the poor. They also recognized problems with GDP measurement for the purposes of measuring development. Amongst other things, Chenery and his co-authors suggested 'weighting' the GNP of the bottom 40 per cent more heavily when calculating growth for development.

The International Labour Organization (ILO) proclaimed, as early as 1944, that poverty anywhere constitutes a 'danger to prosperity everywhere'. In 1976 it advocated for a *basic needs approach* to address poverty, stating that the goal of development was to satisfy the most basic needs of all people in the shortest possible time. For the ILO, increasing employment was required to address basic needs. These basic needs were identified as what people require to live their lives—food, clean water, shelter, clothing, and access to essential health care, education, and transport. More sophisticated versions of the basic needs approach moved beyond the provision of specific goods and services in an effort to embrace broader social achievements such as nutrition and health, literacy, and longevity.

Amartya Sen, Paul Streeten, Mahbub ul Haq, and others argued that development provides for the possibility of living a fuller life. They saw the prior focus on prices and production as an incomplete means to address fundamental human needs. The focus on human development and well-being provided a different perspective to development from not only the neo-classical approaches but also from the 'Marxist' focus on unequal power or class relations between and within countries.

People-Centred Development

The concept of *human development* takes the insights of the *basic needs approach* and adds the concept of well-being and capabilities. Since 1990 the United Nations *Human Development Report* has produced annual comparative data and analysis which seeks to go beyond purely economic data to provide a people-centred analysis of development. The 1996 Report identified five types of growth failure: jobless growth, ruthless growth (only a small group benefit), voiceless growth (lacking democracy or empowerment, particularly for women), rootless growth (cultural identity undermined), and futureless growth (resources and environment not conserved for future generations).

The human development approach goes beyond widely available social indicators, by indexing a set of indicators—including mortality and morbidity rates, school enrolment and literacy rates—to provide a broader perspective of development outcomes. To capture this approach, the Human Development Index (HDI) includes measures of health, education, and standards of living. GDP and HDI can be used in conjunction to provide different insights into development; two countries with the same GDP per capita may have very different HDI rankings. Although the HDI moves beyond GDP, it is important to remember that it is only a partial measure of human development at best, as it relies on a subset of social indicators.

There is no one perfect measure of development, with each of the many measurement tools remaining both conceptually and empirically inadequate. The conceptual shortcomings are compounded by the absence of reliable data. Data quality is weak even in many advanced economies, but on many development dimensions it is almost non-existent—especially for many of the poorest countries. Where it exists, it is often out of date, partial, or inaccurate. Over half of the countries included in the Millennium Development Goals (MDGs) were unable to be accurately reported on, for over half of the targets. Improving national statistical capacity is therefore an urgent requirement, not least in the poorest countries where the needs are great and yet the data is weakest.

This widening and deepening of development analysis to build multidimensional approaches to development builds on Amartya Sen's Capability Approach. This approach recognizes that development is not about income in itself. It is about the freedom people have to achieve valuable ends or what they can 'do' or 'be' with the income at their disposal. Sen showed that people typically differ in their capacity to convert a given income or bundle of resources into similar capabilities and freedoms. A manual labourer, pregnant woman, or person with a parasitic disease may require more food to be properly nourished. It follows that if we're concerned with people rather than things, then development must be about the expansion of each individual's capabilities.

A key question in development is whose experiences matter and who can best identify development needs? Participatory notions of development examine how development strategies are formed and implemented. Robert Chambers has posed the question *whose reality counts?* His initial answer was 'to put the last first': children before adults, poor before the rich, weak before the powerful. The implication is a bottom-up, rather than the traditional top-down approach. Involving local communities in decision-making to identify pressing local needs and maximize valuable local capabilities requires decentralizing development policies. It also requires having political representation and levels of community engagement and literacy which can engage in a wide range of decisions regarding development options. For Sen, this is part of what is implied in the quest for 'development as freedom', which is facilitated by democratic institutions, public reason, and popular pressure for positive social change.

Development Indicators

Combining different economic, social, and other indicators to provide composite indices raises many methodological and conceptual questions, not least with respect to the assumptions and weights given to different dimensions of development and their measurement. A simpler option is to provide information on a variety of these indicators in a development matrix. A well-known example is the MDGs agreed by the United Nations member states in 2000. The twenty-one time-bound and measurable targets and sixty indicators associated with the attainment of the eight MDGs are tracked, but not weighted and combined, to measure progress until the end of 2015. Their successor, the Sustainable Development Goals (SDGs) agreed in

September 2015, is even more ambitious, with 17 goals, and 169 targets with multiple indicators (see Chapter 5; see also Box 3 and Box 4 for lists of the goals). The growing number of goals, targets, and indicators reflects our broadening understanding of development priorities as well as the increasing voice of a growing number of stakeholders in development. The difficulty of managing multiple ambitious objectives has invited criticism including with respect to the achievability, complexity, measurability, and prioritization of the multiple objectives.

The Organisation for Economic Cooperation and Development's (OECD) Better Life Index is another contribution to broader measurement. This has eleven indicators: housing, income, jobs, community, education, environment, civic engagement, health, life satisfaction, safety, and work–life balance. These are intended to provide a more nuanced view of what it means to live a better or fulfilled life. The *World Happiness Report* also takes several variables into account: GDP per capita, social support, healthy life expectancy at birth, freedom to make life choices, generosity (including benevolence and voluntarism), and perceptions of corruption. This report has its origins in renewed interest from across the social sciences in subjective components of well-being. The expansion of long-term data sets (such as the *World Value Surveys*) and the growth of new sources of information (most notably, the World Gallup Poll) on 'happiness' and 'life satisfaction' that now covers several poor countries means that subjective well-being indicators are likely to play a more significant role in development analysis in the future.

These OECD and United Nations initiatives build on the 2010 Commission on the Measurement of Economic Performance and Social Progress, set up by French President Nicolas Sarkozy. The Commission, which was chaired by Joseph Stiglitz, in collaboration with Amartya Sen and others, made a compelling case for the need to move beyond economic measures to include both objective and subjective measures that have a profound impact on peoples' lives. In addition to the subjective concepts of well-being, satisfaction, and happiness, the Commission identified factors that impact the quality of life, including health, education, personal activities, political voice and governance, social connections, environmental conditions, personal insecurity, and economic insecurity.

The failure of economic models and markets to account for 'externalities', or to adequately value 'public goods' such as clean air or water, is the subject of increasing debate; as are questions of the sustainability of development trajectories. This is part of a growing interest in *sustainable development* which is discussed in greater depth in Chapter 6.

New Concepts of Development

Our understanding of what development means has changed considerably in the past seventy years. The concept now brings together economic, psychological, and environmental notions of development to meet physical, emotional, and social needs. Scholarly debate and policy experience have been accompanied by a transformation of values and ideals. Together these have contributed to a shift from a narrow focus on economic growth, to broader concepts of basic needs and human freedom.

We need new concepts and indicators which go beyond GDP or HDI to adequately measure sustainable development and to capture the implications of current decisions for future generations. Tools are regularly being added to the different development toolboxes. For example, the Index of Sustainable Economic Welfare factors environmental costs and degradation into measures of expenditure and service provision. The Happy Planet Index combines experienced well-being (life satisfaction) with life expectancy and a country's ecological footprint. According to this metric, Mexico is ranked higher than its wealthy northern neighbours, due to its smaller ecological footprint.

Our understanding of development will undoubtedly continue to evolve, reflecting new concerns and challenges. Scholars are only just beginning to address the needs of integrating climate and other concerns regarding systemic risks into the literature. Climate change, like the growing threat posed by health challenges, including diabetes and obesity and antibiotic resistance, are among the new development challenges which have arisen as a consequence of development success.

The different dimensions of inequality and their consequences are not well understood. Inequalities in income and wealth are receiving growing attention. However, gender inequality, and inequality based on race, religion, creed, age, disability, and sexual preferences remain profound dividers in most societies, even though they are often barely recognized. Some progress has been made in terms of measures—

most notably with the introduction of the gender-adjusted HDI and inequality-adjusted HDI. Development has also been associated with changing perceptions regarding discrimination. Gender and racial equality are now codified in law in several countries, even though this does not yet translate into equality of opportunity, pay, or other outcomes. Same-sex or gay marriage is now recognized in more than eighteen countries, including a number of developing countries such as South Africa and Uruguay. While the understanding of discriminatory practices is evolving, the necessary actions to address inequalities based on discriminatory practices are lagging everywhere, providing a development challenge in even the most advanced societies.

Growing inequality in almost all societies is reflected by the coexistence of the challenge of dealing with spillovers, such as climate change, arising from rapid growth and improvements in living standards, as well as, the continued challenge of dire poverty. We need to be concerned with both relative and absolute deprivation as well as the sustainability of development. Development thinking has come a long way, but there are still numerous areas that require new and innovative thought if we are to successfully address the remaining intractable old challenges as well as the rapidly emerging new development challenges.

2

⸺ oœo ⸺

How Does Development Happen?

Our understanding of how development happens has evolved. As development thinking has progressed, the categories used to describe countries and different stages or states of 'development' have also evolved (see Box 1).

BOX 1 *Evolving typologies of countries*

Developed	Developing
Advanced	Emerging
Mature	Frontier
Highly Developed	Least Developed
High Income	Low Income
Rich	Poor
Developed	Underdeveloped
Industrial	Non-Industrial
First World	Third Word
Centre	Periphery

The first phase of the evolution of post-war development theory was strongly influenced by classical writings on political economy which date back to the eighteenth century. Among the most influential of the early pioneers of development thinking were Adam Smith, Karl Marx, David Ricardo, Thomas Malthus, and John Stuart Mill.

Smith's famous 1776 book, *The Wealth of Nations*, focuses on the economic development of England. For Smith, the *progress of opulence* was driven by the growth of labour and stock of capital. Efficiency improvements, arising out of the division of labour and adoption of new technologies, were associated with the expansion of markets and foreign trade.

In 1817, Ricardo developed a theory of *comparative advantage* to show that as long as countries specialize in producing goods and services according to their relative efficiencies— in terms of labour productivity—they will benefit from trade even if they do not have an absolute advantage.

In 1820, following on from Smith and Ricardo, Malthus emphasized *growth retarding factors* as well as the limits to population growth. He argued that an increase in population would lead to more impoverished workers with limited purchasing power, and that higher population growth did not generate effective demand and wealth creation. Malthus rejected the prevailing wisdom articulated in Jean-Baptiste Say's argument in 1803 that demand always responds to supply, arguing instead that societies could enter long periods of stagnation.

Marx identified five stages in the development of human societies in a historically deterministic process. The first, known as primitive communism, is characterized by shared property, in which tribes live communally and have no concept of ownership. The second stage, slavery, is associated with the emergence of classes, states that enforce rules, and private property. Marx identified the middle ages in Europe as a transition to the third stage of feudalism that arises after a titled aristocracy—often associated with religious rule—takes power. He argued that the growth of a merchant class threatens the feudal order and leads to conflicts, such as The French Revolution of 1789 and English Civil Wars of 1642 and 1688. Societies then enter the fourth phase of capitalism, which is characterized by a market economy and private property with the profit motive. This leads to imperialism, monopolistic tendencies, and the exploitation of wage-earning workers who no longer control the means of production. Marx envisaged the next socialist stage would arise from growing class consciousness among workers who seize their factories, banks, and other 'commanding heights' of the economy. The further evolution of socialism into a truly communist stage of development was seen by Vladimir Lenin, a Russian communist revolutionary, politician, and political theorist, and others' interpretations of Marx, as the ultimate stage of development.

In 1848, at around the same time that Marx was writing, Mill also looked at the conditions of production and possibilities of social change. Like Marx, and in certain respects Malthus, he too considered the limitations of economic growth and consequences of population growth. However, Mill had a different perspective on the interaction of economic developments with environmental protection and the relation between personal liberty, women's rights, and the strengths and pitfalls of democratic representation. He was among the first to argue that growth may need to be curtailed in the interests of protecting the environment and also was one of the first men to argue with conviction and clarity against the 'subjection of women'. (In 1823 Mill was arrested for distributing pamphlets on birth control and spent a night in jail.)

What these and other classical authors have in common is that, firstly, they were all concerned with the evolution of societies from largely feudal and rural to principally urban and industrial, secondly that they believed that capital accumulation and the expansion of wealth was necessary, and thirdly that they suggested that there is only one single trajectory of development that all countries follow. Many of these assumptions were challenged at the time, and subsequently, with the added benefit of hindsight, have proven inadequate.

Notions of Modernization

In the 1950s and 1960s, *Modernization Theory* attempted to identify commonalities in the process of development in highly developed countries. Overall, economic development was seen to be marked by: a move away from subsistence—food no longer makes up such a large proportion of domestic private consumption of goods; demographic shifts—lower mortality rates, followed by a decline in birth rates; urbanization; and an expansion of both domestic and international trade.

Some economists considered the trajectory of development as influenced by the initial structure or conditions of an economy. Economists believed that specialization patterns are determined by country size, the availability of labour, capital, land, and natural resources, and the relationship to other countries.

Modernization theorists such as Talcott Parsons, Daniel Lerner, and David McClelland, influenced by the work of Max Weber and Emile Durkheim, argued that development required not only particular economic characteristics, but also the social and psychological characteristics of a country. They saw modernization as a *cultural* process, and argued that development is contingent on modern social and cultural values and norms: in order to develop, the norms of modern society must supplant those of traditional societies.

Modernization, according to the theory, could occur through the diffusion of ideas, norms, values, attitudes, and policies in the so-called 'Third World'—now referred to as *developing countries*. These modern values would encourage industrial development and growth and, they argued, development could not occur without them. Despite being largely discredited in recent decades, modernization theory strongly influenced Western governments' development policies in the 1950s and 1960s and was associated with encouraging international trade, reducing aid programmes, and promoting the 'modern' values of entrepreneurship. The idea that development is a distinctly Western experience—or that modernization must follow the same path that Western countries took, with a unique end state which follows the Western model—was subject to growing criticism. By the 1980s, there was widespread rejection of a number of the central tenets of modernization theory.

Critics argued that the generalization of 'traditional' and 'modern' societies made by modernization theorists failed to account for historical and country-specific evidence. 'Traditional' norms and values can adapt to the processes of modernization or even be reinforced by them. For example, kinship ties are not obliterated by modernity but survive in distinct forms in modern cultures. Traditional patterns can also be drawn upon to encourage economic development. Modernization theory has been largely rejected as simplistic in its reliance on norms and traditions to explain development and its neglect of historical or structural evidence. The greatest flaw in modernization theory has been its disregard for the history of colonization and the legacy of imperialism that in many countries reversed key dimensions of development, creating poverty and destitution where there previously had been flourishing societies.

Planning for Economic Development

In the period after the Second World War another group of economists similarly gained inspiration from the classical economists' characterization of immutable economic stages. They drew on experiences gleaned from Franklin D. Roosevelt's New Deal which helped the United States escape the Great Depression, and their observations regarding the increased role of the state during and after the Second World War, to introduce concepts of a *big push* in development that translated into activist investment and policy programmes.

These pioneers of post-war development theory placed a strong emphasis on rigidities in resource allocation and incomplete or missing markets as impediments to development. In these models, industrialization and development are held back by structural factors that lead to uneven power relations. These include declining terms of trade, the economies of scale in manufacturing and infrastructure (so called technical indivisibilities), fragmented investment efforts which do not reach scale, and population growth which places downward pressure on agricultural wages and productivity. Government intervention was therefore seen as necessary to prevent the economies becoming trapped in a low level equilibrium and to enable competitive domestic industries to emerge by providing critical infrastructure, protection for infant industries, and support for economic and political institutions. Examples of such intervention included the creation of state marketing boards and state-owned enterprises which could compete with multinational firms, as well as active engagement by governments in labour, property and other markets, and in trade.

Paul Rosenstein-Rodan was among the first to articulate an explicit development agenda in his 1943 article 'Problems of Industrialisation of Eastern and South-Eastern Europe'. He highlighted the need for a big push to get development going. This he believed could be achieved through large-scale planned investment in industry in post-war economies and by taking advantage of surplus labour which would leave agriculture, as it and industry became more mechanized and benefited from economies of scale. While the focus was on Europe, the theory was all enveloping with Rosenstein-Rodan suggesting that such processes could ultimately equalize world incomes.

In 1953, Ragnar Nurkse's *Problems of Capital Formation in Underdeveloped Countries* emphasized the importance of capital accumulation and advocated the theory of the big push to break the vicious cycle of poverty in developing countries. The crux of the problem, for Nurkse, was that capital accumulation is held back by the size of the market. Poor countries remained poor due to vicious circle of poverty which needed to be unlocked through a big push of investment. His 'law of balanced growth' requires simultaneous investment in multiple industries and sectors to enlarge markets, increase productivity, and create incentives for private enterprises.

W. Arthur Lewis strongly influenced development thinking. In 1954, he argued that a rise in the rate of investment is required for the transition to growth. According to Lewis the central challenge in economic development is increasing the rate of capital accumulation and investment. For Lewis this implied that the key question is how a community which was previously saving, and investing, 4 or 5 per cent of its national income or less, converts itself into an economy where voluntary saving is running at about 12 to 15 per cent of national income or more. In the Lewis *dual-sector model* a shift in resources from the subsistence to the modern sector increases profits and raises savings, and thus investment.

A few years later, in 1960, Walt Rostow published *The Stages of Economic Growth: A Non-Communist Manifesto*, in which he identified distinct stages of development. These were: firstly, traditional society, secondly the preconditions for take-off, thirdly the take-off, fourthly the drive to maturity, and fifthly the age of high mass consumption. His account emphasized the composition of investment, the growth of particular sectors, and sought to identify 'leading sectors' to advance the economy. For Rostow, the take-off stage is the turning point and occurs when economic activity reaches a critical level and leads to: a rise in productive investment from around 5 to about 10 per cent of national income; the development of a high-growth manufacturing sector; and the emergence of social, political, and institutional arrangements that support the modern sector.

In 1958, Albert Hirschman identified the importance of certain industries which have particularly dense linkages with other industries. The implication was that promoting such industries—such as automobile and steel—would enable the economy to grow faster. For Hirschman the goal was to encourage 'unbalanced growth', and investment in industries with the greatest number of 'forward' and 'backward' linkages. He argued that development depends not so much on finding optimal combinations for given resources and factors of production as on enlisting for development purposes resources and abilities that are not yet evident or dispersed or poorly utilized. Hirschman identified four types of linkages: *Forward* linkages when investment in a particular project encourages investment in subsequent stages of production. *Backward* linkages when projects encourage investment in infrastructure and suppliers of goods and services that provide the inputs for the project to succeed. *Consumption* linkages when rising incomes stimulate the production of consumer goods. And *fiscal* linkages when surpluses arising from one sector, such as agriculture, are taxed by the government to promote industrial development. These linkages were seen as powerful arguments to support notions of import substitution industrialization and for state intervention to protect and nurture 'infant' industries.

Dependency Theory

Arguments in favour of import substitution industrialization were reinforced by a trade pessimism articulated at a United Nations Conference in Havana in 1949 by Hans Singer in his paper on 'Post-war Price Relations between Under-developed and Industrialized Countries'. At the same conference, Raúl Prebisch presented his *Manifesto*. Singer and Prebisch argued that the terms of trade between primary goods and manufacturers were destined to decline over the long term, leaving developing countries dependent on the export of raw materials and agricultural products at a growing disadvantage. Prebisch popularized what became known as *dependency theory* in which development requires a transformation in relations between countries at the *centre* (notably the United States and Europe) and the *periphery* (developing countries). The implication was that the only way in which countries could escape the trap of declining terms of trade and underdevelopment was to end their dependence on the advanced economies by stopping the import of manufactured goods and export of primary goods. A related concern was that foreign firms and investors were seen to be highly exploitative, extracting resources and transferring value out of the country. The desire to protect local firms together with barriers to the repatriation of profits were associated with a growing hostility to transnational corporations (or multinational corporations) and provided a justification for the nationalization of foreign assets.

What became known as the Singer-Prebisch hypothesis challenged Ricardo and the neo-classical views of comparative advantage, by arguing that if left to the market, developing countries would be condemned to permanent poverty and that the world would suffer from increasingly *unequal development*. The term unequal development was originally popularized by Lenin in the early twentieth century and taken up by Leon Trotsky, a Marxist Russian revolutionary and theorist, in subsequent decades, and then later by Samir Amin, Andre Gunder Frank, Immanuel Wallerstein, and others in support of what became known as the neo-Marxist or *structuralist* approaches to 'Third World' development (with the First World being the advanced capitalist economies and the Second World the Soviet Union and its closely aligned countries).

Arguments for import substitution industrialization had particular traction in Latin America. This was reflected in Prebisch's appointment in 1950 as the head of the Economic Commission for Latin America (ECLA, which became the Economic Commission for Latin America and the Caribbean or ECLAC, an organization known more widely by its Spanish acronym CEPAL). Prebisch and others at

ECLAC became highly influential in a succession of Latin American and later South Asian and African countries that were determined to end the perceived hold of the advanced economies on their development prospects. These policies were seized upon by leaders of the newly independent countries following the wave of decolonization in the late 1950s and early 1960s. In 1964, the broader appeal of such *structuralist* policies was evident in the establishment of a new United Nations agency and the appointment of Prebisch as the founding Secretary-General of the United Nations Conference on Trade and Development.

Neo-Classical Market-Led Development

By the late 1970s and early 1980s a range of factors led to the pendulum swinging sharply to the right, away from a statist approach to development. Among the reasons for this reaction were the following. First, in many developing countries, and in the Soviet Union, and other centrally planned economies, statist policies had failed to produce the desired development results. Second, in many countries protected state-owned enterprises and industries failed to mature and required continued protection and subsidies. Third, the insulation of domestic industries from international competition, trade, and investment had meant that protected industries fell behind, as increasingly out-of-date technologies and products persisted.

Fourth, policies of the planning era were associated with what became known as *rent-seeking* behaviour. This is when an individual, firm, or organization uses lobbying or other means to obtain economic benefits which are not the outcome of productive activity, but rather result in the reallocation of existing resources or profits. Protection offered by tariffs on imported goods, or licenses which prevented the erosion of monopolistic firms benefited a small number of increasingly wealthy and powerful producers at the cost of consumers. As the interests of the few increasingly dominated politics, rising inequality and crony capitalism were seen as a growing obstacle to development.

Fifth, despite their leftist origins, in much of Latin America, Asia, and Africa, the policies of import substitution industrialization had been adopted by autocratic and military dictatorships (including by the apartheid government in South Africa). The tide of democratization which swept across most developing countries had by the 1980s (and early 1990s in Eastern Europe) become associated with a need to widen ownership and increase the role of individuals and small firms rather than the state and monopolistic enterprises in economic decision-making.

Sixth, the leadership of Margaret Thatcher (1979–90) in the United Kingdom, Ronald Reagan (1981–89) in the United States, and Helmut Kohl (1982–89) in Germany was associated with an ideological shift away from state-led growth towards the free market, which in turn was reflected in a change in the policies of national and international institutions such as the World Bank and International Monetary Fund (IMF).

Seventh, the oil price shocks of the 1970s compounded the deficits of many developing countries and resulted in deepening balance-of-payments crises. As a result of these factors, by the 1980s a growing number of countries were suffering economic collapse, with the symptoms including hyperinflation and ballooning budget deficits. Due to the absence of alternative sources of funding they were forced to accept harsh terms from international lenders, who exercised an effective stranglehold on domestic policies. 'Structural adjustment' packages were imposed by the international lenders as a condition of economic bailout packages, heralding a new phase of development dominated by what John Williamson in 1989 labelled as the *Washington Consensus*.

A group of neo-classical economists which included Anne Krueger, who was appointed World Bank Chief Economist, Peter Bauer, Deepak Lal and Jagdish Bhagwati were associated with policies which sought to establish the primacy of free markets (see Box 2). From 1990, with the collapse of the Soviet Union, and in implementing structural adjustment programmes in Africa, Latin America, and Asia, this influential group of economists argued that it was necessary for governments to open markets, engage in trade reform, establish property rights, and roll-back regulations which restricted free enterprise, while dismantling state-owned enterprises and marketing boards and privatizing a wide range of state-owned agencies. Drawing on the Harrod-Domar Model and the Solow Growth Models they argued that closed economies with low saving rates grow more slowly in the short term than open economies with international trade, foreign investment, and higher saving rates. They insisted that the market mechanism allocates resources

BOX 2   *The neo-classical counter-revolution*

The neo-classical development economists argued for the:

a. End of fixed price controls for agricultural products to encourage farmers to produce more

b. Devaluation of exchange rates to foster export-orientated industries, reduce imports, and improve the balance of payments

c. Ending of deliberate attempts to hold down interest rates, so that interest rates would rise to encourage savings and reduce the unproductive allocation of capital

d. Reduction of trade union power, removal of minimum wages, and other protections which they claimed contributed to high wages in manufacturing and the public sector and an urban bias in development

e. Deregulation and the removal of quotas and subsidies, marketing boards, and reductions in tariffs and other barriers to domestic and international free trade

f. Privatization of state-owned enterprises

more efficiently than governments. To achieve development, it was argued that government should be kept to a minimum and markets should be liberalized. For the advocates of this approach, the central task was to ensure that governments 'got out of the way' of development and allowed the markets to work. A key element in aligning incentives was to 'get the prices right' by eliminating exchange and price controls in developing countries. Lal expressed this new orthodoxy by stating that imperfect markets are superior to imperfect planning and that the most serious current distortions in many developing economies are not those flowing from the inevitable imperfections of a market economy but rather the policy-induced distortions created by 'irrational dirigisme' where states exert an excessive influence over investment.

Trade liberalization was seen as an engine for growth in that it was seen to widen markets, promote international competition, increase employment and incomes, and transfer skills and technology. Drawing on the Ricardo and Hecksher-Ohlin trade theories, the neo-classical advocates of trade reform argued that opening up an economy to international trade results in a new set of relative prices, corresponding changes in the structure of production, and raising the output potential of an economy.

The combination of ideological convergence in the leading advanced countries around a strongly market-based approach, together with the heightened power of the global institutions, as a result of the debt crisis and collapse of Soviet influence, meant that by the early 1990s a growing number of developing countries had relinquished the statist 1960s model of development and shifted to market-led approaches.

Chile, the former Soviet Union, together with Ghana, Kenya, and a number of other African countries (subject to structural adjustment programmes at the time), provided the experimental test bed for the new neo-classical approach to development. The result was far from positive. History, does not provide a counterfactual, so while it is clear that the policies did little to restore growth and development, the alternatives may have been no better, given the dire straits of the economies which were forced to endure the adjustment programmes. By 1995, according to World Bank indicators, thirty-seven sub-Saharan countries had received structural adjustment loans. GNI per capita in the region fell by 27 per cent from $668 in 1980, when the first programmes were put in place to $482 when they were abandoned in 2002.

The State and Market

In the 1990s the growing recognition that markets alone cannot deliver development engendered a rich debate on the role of the state and market. As part of this, the importance of institutions and governance, as well as education, health, and infrastructure, which had been neglected and undermined by free market fundamentalists, was restored. As the ideological pendulum began to swing back towards the centre, the challenge of ensuring an effective interplay between the state and markets was seen to lie at the heart of development. The failure of the economic liberalization and the structural adjustment programmes imposed on developing countries, and the failure of the substitution of the market for the state to provide positive developmental outcomes in the Soviet Union, led to growing disillusionment with the neo-classical doctrines which prevailed in the 1980s.

Academic contributions, politics, and policymakers inter-acted and a new consensus gradually started to emerge. The painful lessons of the debt crises of the 1970s, 1980s, and 1990s were learnt. The affected countries were determined to get their houses in order and not to return cap in hand to the IMF and the World Bank. The result was a growing recogni-tion of the need to premise development policies on solid macroeconomic foundations. By the mid-1990s the major-ity of developing countries had converged around the need for orthodox macroeconomic policies in terms of interest rates, taxes, spending, and inflation and had escaped the cycle of economic crises which had characterized the previ-ous two decades (average government deficits and inflation rates in developing countries since 1990 have been well under half the levels that prevailed in the 1970s and 1980s).

While supporting sound macroeconomic policies, the World Bank and other international development institu-tions have helped swing the pendulum away from a narrow reliance on markets to broader development objectives. The role of education, health, water, energy, transport, and other infrastructure is seen as increasingly important. So too is the development of institutions of governance—including judi-ciary and legal systems—national and municipal represen-tative structures, and the media.

The global convergence of development thinking around a new consensus on the importance of both states and markets and the need for an alignment of donors and recipients' interests was articulated in September 2000 at a conference in Mexico at which 147 heads of state and representatives of 187 countries signed the *Millennium Declaration*. This envisaged a global partnership for development—at the national and global level—which would further development and support the elimination of poverty. The Declaration laid the foundation for a new phase of development activities articulated in the MDGs.

3

⊶∞⊷

Why Are Some Countries Rich and Others Poor?

There is a great deal of variation in the development experience of different countries. Why have some countries experienced a growth 'miracle' while others have experienced what can be described as a growth 'tragedy'?

Uneven Development

Theories of economic growth have tended to predict that the per capita incomes of all economies will converge over time. Among the best known and most widely used is the model developed by Robert Solow in 1956. Growth in the model is essentially determined by increasing capital investments, arising from raising savings rates, and by the growth in the labour force. The model was used to predict that to the extent poor countries are able to achieve savings rates which are similar to the rich countries, they will catch up with them. The Solow Model, like all economic models, although highly influential, is stylized, providing a fertile foundation for subsequent generations of economists.

In 1986, William Baumol compared the long-term growth rates of sixteen countries that are now amongst the richest in the world. He found strong evidence of convergence over the period from 1870 to 1979. Baumol has been criticized for selection bias in his statistical analysis as he only considered countries that are rich today—such as Japan—and excluded countries that did not converge—such as Argentina which failed to catch up. Later studies attempted to avoid selection bias by including additional countries that would have been good candidates for membership of a 'convergence club' in 1870—the result is that the statistical evidence for convergence is much weaker.

In contrast to theoretical arguments regarding convergence, a number of economists have pointed to divergent GDP growth over the long run. Angus Maddison painstakingly assembled the longest and largest number of comparable country historical records. His statistics can be used to analyse the long-run growth of a wide range of countries (see Figure 1 and Figure 2). For example, his data shows that in 1908 Argentina had a GDP per capita of \$3,657 (ranked 7th in the world), which exceeded that of Netherlands, Canada, Denmark, Austria, Germany, and France. Uruguay (\$2,973, ranked 14th) was not too far behind. But by 2010 Argentina only had a GDP per capita of \$10,256 and was ranked 43rd in the world and Uruguay (\$11,526, ranked 39th) had also lost ground. These countries were overtaken by most Western European and a number of other countries.

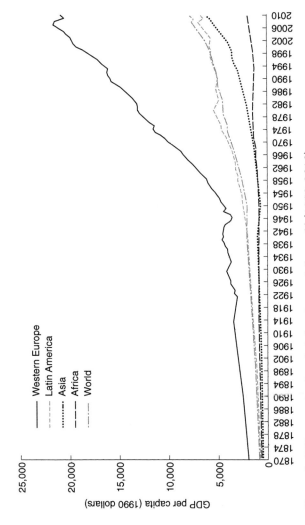

Figure 1 GDP per capita for selected regions and the world (1870–2010).

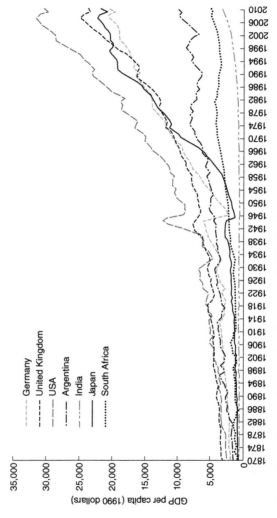

Figure 2 GDP per capita for selected countries (1870–2010).

By contrast Japan only had a per capita income of $737 in 1870 (ranked 38th), and $2,873 in 1941 (ranked 21st), but by 2010 per capital income reached $21,935 (ranked 17th). And Hong Kong had a per capita income of $683 in 1870 (ranked 44th), $1,279 in 1913 (ranked 33rd) and $30,725 (ranked 1st) in 2010.

The divergence appears to have been particularly marked since the Second World War. For example, data collected from 1960 shows that while Ghana has failed to double its per capita income over the last half a century ($766 in 2014), South Korea ($24,566 in 2014) has increased real per capita income by a factor of 22 over the same period. Only China performed better than South Korea.

Seven countries experienced a decline in real per capita income between 1960 and 2014 and a further twenty-four countries failed to double per capita income over the same period, whereas fourteen countries increased per capita income by at least a factor of 5—five of these by a factor of over 10, and two by a factor of over 20. The vast majority managed to increase real per capita income by a factor of 2 or 3.

Overall, the evidence points to divergence—rather than convergence—in recent decades, although there is some variation amongst geographical sub-groupings, with a set of Southeast Asian economies (the 'tigers') displaying evidence of convergence. In 1993, Parente and Prescott studied 102 countries over the period from 1960 to 1985. They found that disparities in wealth between rich and poor countries persist, although there is some evidence of dramatic divergence within Asia, which is consistent with some South East Asian economies—Japan, Taiwan, South Korea, and Thailand—catching up with the West. Li and Xu, have highlighted the extent to which the real incomes of seven South East Asian economies have grown 3.5 times (Malaysia) to 7.6 times (China) faster than the United States and the G10 economies in the period from 1970 to 2010.

The World Bank attributed the 'East Asian Miracle' to sound macroeconomic policies with limited deficits and low debt, high rates of savings and investment, universal primary and secondary education, low taxation of agriculture, export promotion, promotion of selective industries, a technocratic civil service, and authoritative leaders. However, the Bank failed to highlight the extent to which the achievements came at the expense of civil liberties, and that far from being free markets the governments concerned subjugated the market (and suppressed organized labour), often with the generous support of the United States and other development and military aid programmes, following the Korean and Vietnam Wars.

Others have argued that South East Asia's relative success had more to do with pursuing strategic rather than 'close' forms of integration with the world economy. In other words instead of opting for unbridled economic liberalization in line with the neo-classical market friendly approach to development, countries such as Japan, South Korea, and Taiwan selectively intervened in the economy in an effort to ensure that markets flourished. Several well-known commentators including Ajit Singh, Alice Amsden, and Robert Wade have documented the full range of measures adopted by these countries, which appear to constitute a purposive and comprehensive industrial policy. These measures include the use of long-term credit (at negative real interest rates), the heavy subsidization and coercion of exports, the strict control of multinational investment and foreign equity ownership of industry (in the case of Korea), highly active technology policies, and the promotion of large-scale conglomerates together with restrictions on the entry and exit of firms in key industrial sectors. The debate continues over the relative contribution to the success of South East Asian economies of selective forms of intervention on the one hand, and market-friendly liberalization and export orientation on the other.

Poverty and Inequality

The number of people below the $1.90 per day (2011 PPP) poverty line was 896 million in 2012, the latest date for which global poverty statistics are available. By 2015 the number is expected to have fallen to 702 million. The 2012 numbers indicate that 14.8 per cent of people living in the developing countries were below the poverty line, down from 44.4 per cent in 1990 and 53.9 per cent in 1981.

In 2012, about 85 per cent of the developing world's population (98 per cent in South Asia, 97 per cent in sub-Saharan Africa, 84 per cent in East Asia and the Pacific, and 65 per cent in Latin America and the Caribbean) lived on less than $13 per day—the official United States poverty line in 2005.

We have shown that income measures are only one dimension of poverty. Other indicators, including those relating to infant and child mortality, illiteracy, infectious disease, malnutrition, and schooling are also important (see Table 1). A number of countries have made extraordinary

Table 1. Selected indicators of poverty and development

	Life expectancy at birth (years) (2013)	Infant mortality rate (per 1,000 live births) (2015)	Adult literacy rate (% older than 15) (2010)	Primary school enrolment (%)* (2013)	DPT immunization (% aged 12–23 months) (2014)
South Asia	66.9	42	66.7	89.5	82.7
East Asia & Pacific	74.0	15	94.5	94.2	92.3
Sub-Saharan Africa	56.8	56	60.3	77.4	77.2
Middle East & North Africa	71.5	21	77.9	93.9	88.1
Latin America & Caribbean	74.6	16	91.5	91.8	88.1
Europe & Central Asia	72.4	18	98.2	92.4	93.6
World	70.9	32	85.2	89.0	85.9
Low income	59.2	53	57.5	79.9	78.5
Middle income	70.1	31	83.4	89.7	86.0

Note:— = no data.
* Net enrolment rate for children of official primary school age. Excludes those attending primary school who are not of primary school age.
Source: World Bank, *World Development Indicators* (online), http://data.world bank.org/ (last accessed 26 September 2015).

	Measles immunization (% 12–23 months) (2014)	Population undernourished (%) (2013)	Access to improved water source (%) (2015)	Access to improved sanitation (%) (2015)	Access to electricity (%) (2012)
South Asia	80.4	16.3	92.4	44.8	78.0
East Asia & Pacific	93.3	10.9	93.7	74.9	95.7
Sub-Saharan Africa	72.7	19.5	67.6	29.7	35.3
Middle East & North Africa	86.2	8.7	92.6	89.7	95.9
Latin America & Caribbean	92.3	8.2	94.2	80.6	95.8
Europe & Central Asia	93.8	—	96.6	93.7	100.0
World	84.5	13.0	91.0	67.5	84.6
Low income	76.9	27.3	65.6	28.2	24.8
Middle income	84.6	11.9	92.0	64.7	87.4

strides in overcoming poverty. In some, progress has been across the board, whereas others have managed to achieve very significant progress on one dimension but fallen back on others, as previously stated.

Inequality between countries and within countries requires an analysis which goes beyond the headline economic indicators. While average per capita incomes are growing in most countries, inequality is also growing almost everywhere. The world's richest 20 per cent of people account for three-quarters of global income and consume about 80 per cent of global resources, while the world's poorest 20 per cent consume well under two per cent of global resources. Where poor people are is also changing. Twenty years ago over 90 per cent of the poor lived in low-income countries; today approximately three-quarters of the world's poorest one billion people live in middle-income countries.

Explaining Different Development Outcomes

We need to be mindful that every country is unique. Yet it is still possible to identify a range of factors that affect development trajectories. A number of economic historians have shown that patterns of *resource endowments* can reinforce inequalities and favour elites, with this in turn leading to 'capture' and predatory institutional development. The *resource curse* has been examined by Paul Collier, Jeffrey Frankel, and others, who have shown that ample endowments of natural resources may be linked with stunted institutional development, particularly in the case of minerals and oil. In the mining and oil sectors, multinational and local investors have often operated behind a veil of secrecy. The awarding of contracts for extractive industries provides a source of power and patronage to corrupt leaders. Evidence of corruption by international firms who have made off-shore payments through international banks provides a clear example of how both advanced and developing countries have a responsibility to clamp down on corrupt practices, not least in mitigating the various risks associated with the extraction of natural resources.

For the classical and neo-classical economists, as well as their critics on the left, natural and human *resource endowments* were a key determinant of trade and market integration. While the former group argued that revealed comparative advantage would lead to development, the critics argued the opposite, concluding that it would lead to more uneven development. Both groups saw international trade as a critical determinant of growth, explaining the convergence (or divergence) of growth rates and global incomes, with Dani Rodrik, Jeffrey Sachs and Andrew Warner, Jeffrey Frankel and David Romer, and David Dollar and Aart Kray contributing conflicting evidence of the relationship between trade and development.

Jared Diamond, Jeffrey Sachs, and others explain development outcomes by providing *geographical explanations*. They argue that moderate advantages or disadvantages in geography can lead to big differences in long-term economic outcomes. Geography is thought to affect growth in at least four ways. Firstly, economies with more coastline, and easy access to sea trade, or large markets have lower transport costs and are likely to outperform economies that are distant and landlocked. Secondly, tropical climatic zones face a higher incidence of infectious and parasitic diseases which hold back economic performance by reducing worker productivity, and indirectly by adding to the demographic burden as a high incidence of disease can raise fertility rates. This is particularly due to high infant mortality, such as arises due to over 1,000 children under five dying of malaria every day in Africa. Thirdly, geographical environments affect agricultural productivity in a variety of ways. Grains are less productive in tropical zones, with a hectare of land in the tropics yielding on average around one-third of the yield in temperate zones. Fragile soils in the tropics and extreme weather are part of the explanation, as is the higher incidence of pests and parasites which damage crops and livestock. Fourthly, as the tropical regions have lower incomes and crop values, agri-businesses invest less in tropical regions, and national research institutions are similarly poorer. The implication is that international agencies, such as the Consultative Group for International Agricultural Research (CGIAR)—which is donor funded—have a particular responsibility to raise the output of tropical agriculture. A similar point can be made with respect to tropical diseases, with low purchasing power holding back development of drugs to combat many of the most significant tropical diseases.

William Easterly and Ross Levine, as well as Rodrik and others, have argued that the impact of geography is regulated through institutions and that good governance and institutions can provide the solution to bad geography. For example, good governments can build efficient roads and irrigation systems, and invest in vital infrastructure as well as enforce legal contracts and curb corruption. Good governance reduces uncertainty and this together with increased investment, can overcome bad geography. As bad geography makes development more difficult, more aid might be required to overcome geographical deficits in the poorest places, as Sachs has emphasized.

Rodrik and others argue that it is the quality of *institutions*—property rights and the rule of law—that ultimately matters. Once the quality of institutions is taken into account (statistically 'controlled for' using econometric techniques), the effect of geography on economic development fades. However, as Rodrik notes, the policy implications associated with the 'institutions rule' thesis are difficult to discern and likely to vary according to context. This in part is because institutions are partly endogenous and co-evolve with economic performance. As countries become better off they have the capacity to invest in more education and skills and better institutions, which in turn makes them better off.

For Daron Acemoglu, Simon Johnson, and James Robinson, the development of institutions which facilitate or frustrate development, are rooted in *colonialism and history*. These authors argue that contemporary patterns of development are largely the result of different forms of colonialism and the manner in which particular countries were, or were not, settled over the past five hundred years. The purposes and nature of colonial rule and settlement shaped institutions which have had lasting impacts. In areas with high disease burdens, high population density, and an abundance of natural resources, colonial powers typically set up 'extractive states' with limited property rights and few checks against government power in order to transfer resources to colonizers, such as was the case in the Belgian Congo. In countries with low levels of disease and low population density, and less easily extractable resources, settlement was more desirable and colonial powers attempted to replicate European institutions in which they could thrive as settlers—strong property rights and checks on the abuse of power—and made an effort to develop agriculture and industry as was the case in Canada, United States, Australia, and New Zealand. According to this thesis, the legacy of colonialism led to an institutional reversal that made poor countries rich, and rich countries poor in a 'reversal of fortune'.

Although we may well live in a world shaped by natural resource endowments, geography, history and institutions, politics and power can still play a decisive role in terms of driving economic performance and determining vulnerability to poverty. In Amartya Sen's *Poverty and Famines*, he showed that political power and rules that are embedded in ownership and exchange determine whether people are malnourished or have adequate food, and that malnourishment is not mainly the result of inadequate food supply. Sen shows how droughts in North Africa, India, and China in the nineteenth and twentieth centuries were catastrophic for social and political reasons, with power relations, not agricultural outcomes, leading to widespread starvation and destruction of the peasantry. In 1979, Colin Bundy, in

The Rise and Fall of the South African Peasantry, was among a new wave of historians who argued that colonialism led to the deliberate collapse of a previously thriving domestic economy. In 1997, Jared Diamond's, *Blood, Germs and Steel*, while emphasizing the importance of geography and history, showed how technology, culture, disease, and other factors led to the destruction of many colonized indigenous populations and other previously thriving communities. These authors, echoing Marx, highlighted the extent to which development can be a very bloody business, even if the longer-term consequences may be to bludgeon societies into a new era.

If the abuse of power can set development back, what about the counter argument that *democracy* leads to more rapid and equitable development outcomes? According to Irma Adelman, the long-term factors governing the association between development and democracy include the growth of middle classes, increase in quantity and quality of education, urbanization (including more infrastructure), the need for participation in development strategies, and the need to manage the psychological and social strains arising from change. Acemoglu, Robinson, and others went further in 2014, arguing that democracy does cause growth, and that it has a significant and robust positive effect on GDP. Their results suggest that democracy increases future GDP by encouraging investment, increasing schooling, and inducing economic reforms, improving public good provision, and reducing social unrest. The difficulty of defining democracy, and the weight attached to the non-democracies which have enjoyed very rapid growth, such as China and Singapore, as well as the slowing of growth and paralysis in decision-making in many parts of Latin America, Europe, and other democratic regions means that the academic jury remains divided on the relationship between development and democracy.

Adelman has argued that democracy cannot persist for any length of time if inequalities amongst groups of citizens are too vast. But, what is the relationship between inequality and development? Albert Hirschman suggested that societies have a changing tolerance for inequality over the course of development. His basic argument is that people are more likely to tolerate a rise in income inequality if they believe this is likely to have positive implications for their own future income. This would allow for a 'grow first, distribute later strategy'.

Simon Kuznets 'inverted-U' hypothesis was based on his empirical observation that relative income inequality tends to rise in the early stages of development, stabilize for a while, and then decline in later stages of development. The resultant 'Kuznets Curve', if plotted on a graph, is an inverted-U shape (Figure 3). From this observation Kuznets surmised that long-term trends in inequality are linked to changes in the structure of the economy. In the early stages the transfer of workers to the industrial sector raises inequalities, but in later stages increases in education and skills, and reductions in population growth over the course of development also provide wide-ranging benefits. However, the Kuznets Curve has been widely criticized, as subsequent studies have shown that inequality can persist over time. In recent decades, inequality between countries appears to be declining, as emerging countries on average have grown

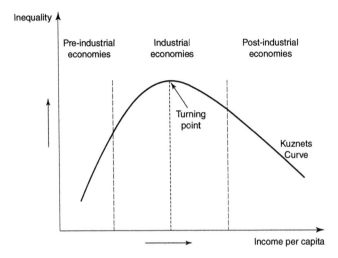

Figure 3 Kuznets Curve.

three times more rapidly than advanced economies. Within virtually all countries, however, inequality is rising. This suggests that in advanced as well as developing countries technological change, trade-opening, reduced welfare spending, and other factors are leading to a greater concentration of the benefits of growth in the hands of a smaller share of the national population.

4

What Can Be Done to Accelerate Development?

The extraordinary diversity of development experiences reveals the many different available pathways that countries have chosen in order to develop. Each requires a determination to succeed and the sacrifice of short-term benefits for longer-term and societal goals. It is hard to accelerate development and the gains can be easily reversed. Conflict and war overturn development, destroying not only lives, but also the infrastructure and cohesion which are fundamental to development. Development cannot be sustained without peace and stability.

Literacy and education—and particularly the role of education for women—are vital, not least in overcoming gender inequities. Greater participation of women in society is a key contributor to declining fertility and improved family nutrition and health. Infrastructure investments, particularly in clean water, sewerage, and electricity, as well as rural roads, also are essential for growth and investment, as they are for achieving improved health outcomes. The rule of law and the establishment of a level playing field, through competition and regulatory policies are vital for facilitating a flourishing private sector. Market capture by monopolies or small elites, often with the connivance of politicians or civil servants, skews development and leads to growing inequality.

No country is an island economically and the way that countries engage with the rest of the world is a key determinant of their development outcomes. The increasing integration of the world—in terms of financial, trade, aid, and other economic flows, as well as health, educational, scientific, and other opportunities—requires an increasingly sophisticated policy capability. So too does the management of the risks associated with increased integration into the global community. The threat posed by pandemics, cyber attacks, financial crises, and climate change and other global developments could derail the best-laid development efforts. Systemic risks have a particularly negative impact on development outcomes, and have negative distributional consequences. The existence of effective policies, or their absence, shapes the harvesting of the upside opportunities and mitigation of the risks arising from globalization.

Literacy, Education, and Health

There are both theoretical and empirical reasons for believing that literacy and education are essential for economic and social development. The education of girls has served to reduce widespread gender inequalities and has improved the relative position of women in poor countries. The education and empowerment of women has consistently been associated with improvements in a range of positive development outcomes, and particularly sharp falls in infant mortality and fertility.

The links between education, health, and development are many and varied; in many contexts 'all good things' (or 'bad things') go together. The *demographic transition* describes how fertility and mortality rates change over the course of economic and social development. In the early or first phase of development birth rates and mortality rates are high due to poor education, nutrition, and healthcare. In such circumstances, characteristic of many developing countries prior to the Second World War, population growth remains low. As living standards, nutrition, and public health improve during the second phase of the transition, mortality rates tend to decline. As birth rates remain high, population growth becomes increasingly rapid. Much of Africa, Asia, and Latin America experienced this trend during the second half of the twentieth century (see Table 2).

Over half the countries in the world, including many developing countries, have now entered the third stage of demographic transition. This is characterized by improvements in education and health along with changes in technology, including the widespread availability of contraceptives, which give women greater choice. In this stage, urbanization and greater female participation in the workforce reduces the economic and social benefit of having children and raises the costs. In the fourth stage

Table 2. World population by regions

	Total population (millions)							Average annual growth rate (%)					
	1980	1990	2000	2010	2015	2030	2050	1980–90	1990–2000	2000–10	2010–15	2025–35	2045–55
World	4,440	5,310	6,127	6,930	7,349	8,501	9,725	1.79	1.67	1.43	1.18	0.82	0.54
Africa	478	632	814	1,044	1,186	1,679	2,478	2.79	2.70	2.54	2.55	2.16	1.71
Asia	2,626	3,202	3,714	4,170	4,393	4,923	5,267	1.99	1.82	1.48	1.04	0.55	0.14
Europe	694	721	725	735	738	734	707	0.39	0.28	0.07	0.08	-0.14	-0.23
Latin America & Caribbean	365	447	527	600	634	721	784	2.02	1.83	1.65	1.12	0.66	0.21
North America	254	281	314	344	358	396	433	0.99	1.04	1.12	0.78	0.58	0.37
Oceania	23	27	31	36	39	47	57	1.61	1.56	1.42	1.54	1.07	0.76

Note: Includes projections for 2030 and 2050 based on the medium variant.
Source: Author's calculation and United Nations, *World Population Prospects: The 2015 Revision* (Department of Economics and Social Affairs Population Division, 2015), custom data acquired from website, http://esa.un.org/unpd/wpp/DataQuery/ (last accessed 3 October 2015).

of the demographic transition, both mortality and birth rates decline to low or stable levels and population growth begins to fall. Many developed countries have passed this stage and now face the prospect of zero or negative population growth. As this trend continues, countries experience a rapid decline in fertility, to below replacement level. The combination of rapidly falling fertility and continued increases in life expectancy leads to rapid increases in median ages, with these projected to double in all regions, except for Africa, in the period to 2050.

Gender and Development

Gender inequalities and unequal power relations skew the development process. In many developing countries women's opportunities for gainful forms of employment are limited to subsistence farming—often without full land ownership rights or access to credit and technology which could alter production relations and female bargaining power. In many societies, women are confined either to secluded forms of home-based production that yield low returns, or to marginal jobs in the informal economy where income is exceptionally low and working conditions are poor. In addition women typically have to endure the 'double burden' of employment and domestic work—the latter includes housework, preparing meals, fetching water and wood, and caring for children—amongst many other tasks. Indeed, worldwide, women tend to work more hours than men when domestic work is included.

A range of studies over the last four decades have shown that households do not automatically pool their resources, and that who earns and controls income can make a major difference to household well-being. Numerous empirical studies examining the relationship between women's market work, infant feeding practices, and child nutrition indicate that the children of mothers with higher incomes and more economic power are better nourished. In the gold mining industry in Africa for example an increase in women's wage-earning opportunities is associated with increased access to healthcare, the halving of infant mortality rates—especially for girls—and a reduction in the acceptance of domestic violence by 24 per cent.

The distribution of benefits and burdens becomes more equitable when women have a stronger voice and more access to education and employment. Improving women's economic opportunities can prove a highly effective way to reduce poverty and improve women's relative position and that of their children. Overall household well-being is likely to be improved by ensuring that more women are enrolled in education, can read, write, and count, and have appropriate skills for jobs. Steps to tackle restrictive cultural norms and laws regarding women's education, participation in the labour force, ownership of land and other assets, inheritance rights, marriage, and freedom to participate in society make important contributions in this regard.

Many of these initiatives are likely to translate into specific sector priorities and policies—for example vocational training, access to cheap transport, and access to saving and credit markets. Women are disadvantaged in the credit market as they typically have no collateral and smaller informal networks, largely due to their relative confinement to the domestic sphere. Innovative microfinance schemes have sought to overcome this by providing flexible loans on favourable terms, often requiring no collateral or with zero interest, for investment in small-scale productive activities—such as rearing chickens or a goat. The most well-known example is the Grameen Bank, which has been providing finance to poor Bangladeshis since the late 1970s. By 2015 cumulative disbursement of loans exceeded $16 billion and the bank had provided loans to over 7 million individuals, 97 per cent of whom are women.

The participation of women in the workplace together with gender differences in pay, promotion, and business leadership are important aspects of empowerment. Political representation and gender disparities in healthcare and education (often reflecting 'boy preference' in many parts of the world) are also key indicators of social progress. Since the introduction of the MDGs in 1990, women in many countries have made progress towards parity with men, although much more still needs to be done (Table 3). Significant progress has been made in terms of tackling female infant mortality and enabling your girls to attend school, although gross disparities between men and women persist across the board. Despite some notable progress, practices which fundamentally constrain women, among the worst of which is female genital mutilation, which affects at least 125 million women in over twenty-nine countries, continue to pose a major development challenge.

Table 3. Gender-related indicators of development

| | Infant mortality rate (per 1,000 births) | | | | Secondary school enrolment (gross %) | | | | Labour force participation rate (% over 15 years of age) | | | | Seats held in parliament by women (%) | |
| | 1990 | | 2015 | | 1990 | | 2013 | | 1990 | | 2013 | | 1990 | 2014 |
	Male	Female	Male	Female	Male	Female	Male	Female	Male	Female	Male	Female		
South Asia	94.7	88.4	42.9	40.8	44.8	25.9	67.5	63.4	85.3	35.9	80.6	30.5	6.3	19.2
East Asia & Pacific	48.0	41.6	16.3	13.5	43.6	34.4	84.6	85.6	84.2	69.4	79.4	62.6	17.2	19.0
Sub-Saharan Africa	116.4	99.6	61.5	50.9	26.7	20.3	46.1	39.5	79.9	58.9	76.5	63.7	—	22.0
Middle East & North Africa	55.1	49.2	22.4	19.0	63.9	47.2	78.2	73.5	76.6	17.5	73.2	20.1	3.7	16.8
Latin America & Caribbean	50.3	41.6	17.4	14.3	72.5	76.7	89.2	94.6	83.1	40.7	80.4	54.6	12.9	28.5
North America	10.2	8.1	6.0	4.9	91.5	91.4	95.5	95.4	75.5	56.5	69.1	56.8	9.3	21.7
Europe & Central Asia	50.4	41.4	19.8	15.7	88.0	82.2	100.0	97.7	73.0	50.1	69.4	46.0	—	18.6
World	66.4	59.0	33.8	29.5	55.4	46.7	76.3	74.1	80.5	52.2	76.7	50.3	12.7	22.2
Developing countries	74.4	66.2	37.5	32.8	48.2	37.4	71.9	69.3	82.9	53.0	78.7	49.6	12.7	20.9
Low income countries	121.2	105.0	57.7	48.2	22.2	14.0	43.7	35.5	84.3	70.0	83.3	72.2	—	22.3

Source: World Bank, *World Development Indicators*, http://data.worldbank.org/ (last accessed 3 October 2015).

Less progress has been made in terms of women's employment in the labour market—especially in Asia where ground has been lost over the last twenty-five years. This may have far reaching implications beyond our concern with fairness and gender justice. A recent speculative study suggests that advancing gender equality in the workplace could add as much as $12 trillion to global GDP by 2025 (assuming every country in the world could match the performance of its fastest improving neighbour in terms of progress towards gender equality). While the advanced economies have the most to gain, developing countries and regions could expect to benefit from significant increases in income by 2025 including India ($0.7 trillion or 11% of GDP), Latin America ($1.1 trillion or 14 per cent of GDP), China ($2.5 trillion or 12 per cent of GDP), sub-Saharan Africa ($0.3 trillion or 12 per cent of GDP), and the Middle East and North Africa ($0.6 trillion or 11 per cent of GDP) (amongst other countries and regions).

Knowing that education, health and nutrition, and gender equity—amongst other things—are important for development is only the start. Developing policies to tackle these issues is a major challenge. In many countries, for example, the failure of education systems relates to a lack of quality rather than quantity of resources spent. In India case studies have catalogued a number of issues including poorly trained and qualified teachers, mindless and repetitive learning experiences, lack of books and learning material, poor accountability of teachers and unions, school days without formal activities, and high rates of absenteeism amongst staff and students. Moreover, improving outcomes is more complex than finding money for school fees or budgets for teachers. Issues such as having appropriate clothes for the walk to school or the availability of single-sex toilets at school can play a decisive role, especially for girls.

Agriculture and Food

Agriculture provides the main source of income and employment for the 70 per cent of the world's poor that live in rural areas. The price and availability of food and agricultural products also dramatically shapes nutrition and the potential to purchase staples for the urban poor.

Policies such as price controls and export restrictions which discriminate against farmers and seek to create cheap urban food by holding down agricultural prices can perversely lead to rising poverty, especially where the bulk of the poor are in the countryside. Low agricultural prices depress rural incomes, as well as the production and supply of food and agricultural products. The urban poor are, however, more politically powerful than the rural poor, not least as they are present in capital cities. An important contributor to the French Revolution of 1789 was the doubling of bread prices, and urban food protests have continued to pose a serious threat to governments.

In many developing countries these artificially depressed agricultural prices discriminate against farmers. By contrast, in many of the more advanced economies—notably in the United States, European Union, and Japan—certain groups of farmers have achieved an extraordinarily protected position. Tariff barriers and quotas which restrict imports, together with production, input subsidies, tax exemptions, and other incentives benefit a small group of privileged farmers at the expense of consumers and taxpayers in the advanced economies (see Chapter 7). This fundamentally undermines the prospects of farmers in developing countries, who are unable to export the products that they would be competitive in, in a freer market. It also makes the prices of these products more volatile on global markets as only a small share of global production is traded so that international markets become the residual onto which excess production is dumped leading to a collapse in world prices, or shortages that result in sharp upward price movements.

An added cause of instability is that the concentration of production in particular geographic areas of the United States and Europe increases the impact of weather-related risks which exacerbates instability in world food prices. Because farmers in many developing countries cannot export protected crops, they are compelled to concentrate their production in crops that are not produced in the advanced economies, and produce coffee, cocoa, and other solely tropical agricultural commodities. This reduces diversification and leads to excessive specialization in these commodities, depressing prices and raising the risks associated with monocultures. The levelling of the agricultural playing field, which has been a key objective of the Doha Development Round of Trade Negotiations, initiated by the World Trade Organization (WTO) in 2001, remains a key objective of development policy (see Chapter 7).

The unevenness of investments in agricultural research and development is another development challenge. Billions of dollars are allocated by governments and private companies to agricultural research that benefits farmers and consumers in the advanced countries, but only a small fraction of research spending is allocated to crops that are essential to the livelihoods of poor people in poor countries. As a result of this market failure, international institutions and foundations have a vital role to play in providing a *public good* by raising agricultural productivity and improving nutrition in developing countries. The CGIAR consortium (consisting of fifteen international food and agricultural research centres) is an example of a development partnership to advance this public good. With funding from the Gates Foundation, World Bank, and numerous bilateral and multilateral agencies, CGIAR supports research into seeds and systems which have been associated with significant agricultural advances in poor countries. These include the Green Revolution in Asia, which led to sharp improvements in rice yields and quality. The yields of staple crops in Africa have not yet benefited from such a revolution and this is a key priority for international agricultural research. Increasing population and the growing pressure on land, water, and other resources, compounded by the impact of climate change, mean that sustaining production improvements is likely to prove a growing challenge. Stepping up global efforts to improve the quantity and quality of agricultural output is an important dimension of the global development agenda.

The widening of our understanding of development has been accompanied by a growing recognition of the importance of nutrition. Small improvements in micronutrients can have a significant impact. These range from the fortification of salt with iodine to other areas, as advocated by the Global Alliance for Improved Nutrition. Excessive consumption of certain products is a growing concern, as is evident in the growing burden of non-communicable diseases, such as heart attacks, strokes, diabetes, and obesity in developing countries. Indeed developing countries account for over half of the global incidence of non-communicable disease and in many developing countries these 'lifestyle' diseases now account for the most fatalities.

Infrastructure

Infrastructure encompasses the basic physical and organizational structures and facilities required for the development of economies and societies. This includes water and sanitation, electricity, transport (roads, railways, and ports), irrigation, and telecommunications. Infrastructure provides the material foundations for development. Investments in infrastructure tend to require very large and indivisible financial outlays and regular maintenance. These investments shape the evolution of cities, markets, and economies for generations and lock in particular patterns of urbanization and water and energy use. Prudent investment in energy and transport infrastructure can have a significant impact on environmental sustainability through ensuring lower emissions, higher efficiency, and resilience to climate change. Investment in sewerage and sanitation, as well as recycling of water, similarly has a vital role to play in reducing water-use and pollution.

Investment in basic infrastructure tends to have a high economic return. A study of four South Asian economies—India, Pakistan, Bangladesh, and Sri Lanka—using panel data for the period 1980–2005, concluded that infrastructure development contributes significantly to output and highlights the importance of mutual feedback between total output and infrastructure development. A 17 per cent rate of return, on average, for agricultural infrastructure projects has been identified by the World Bank for its projects. According to a survey conducted by the Federation of Indian Chambers of Commerce in 2013, which covered 650 industries, frequent power outages—more than ten hours each week—are taking a toll on production and costing Indian companies up to 40,000 rupees ($733) per day each. It makes sense, then, that investments to overcome critical infrastructure backlogs yield high returns.

Financing infrastructure in developing countries is challenging given the scale of investment required and the corresponding risk factors. These include the fact that large upfront risk capital is often required for the construction phase and that many infrastructure projects face uncertainty regarding future revenue streams associated with policy change, macroeconomic instability, and the affordability of end-user fees. These and other factors mean that governments have a critical role to play in investments in infrastructure as well as in establishing a predictable long-term regulatory and policy framework for private investment which can provide investors with assurance that their investments will be secure over a time horizon extending over several decades.

It has been estimated that investment in infrastructure—excluding operation and maintenance—in developing countries needs to double from its current levels of close to $1 trillion to over $2 trillion per year or from around 3 per cent of GDP currently to 6–8 per cent of GDP by 2020 (see Figure 4). This includes $200 to $300 billion per annum to ensure lower carbon emissions and resilience to climate change.

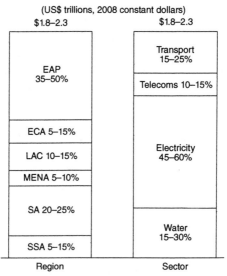

(US$ trillions, 2008 constant dollars)

Region $1.8–2.3	Sector $1.8–2.3
EAP 35–50%	Transport 15–25%
	Telecoms 10–15%
ECA 5–15%	Electricity 45–60%
LAC 10–15%	
MENA 5–10%	
SA 20–25%	
SSA 5–15%	Water 15–30%

Note: EAP = East Asia and Pacific; ECA = Europe and Central Asia; LAC = Latin America and Caribbean; MENA = Middle East and North Africa; SA = South Asia; SSA = sub-Saharan Africa. The figures refer to capital investment only in US dollars (real 2008 prices) and exclude operation and maintenance costs.

Figure 4 Annual infrastructure spending requirements in the developing world.

These aggregate figures hide wide disparities in the magnitude of investment required in different countries and regions and in the requirements of different sectors: energy, water, and transport have the highest requirements. Currently over half of infrastructure in developing countries is financed domestically, with the balance financed by international institutions such as the World Bank and regional development banks. This international finance will need to play a larger role, if the infrastructure deficit is to be overcome, which is why new initiatives, such as the Asian Infrastructure Investment Bank, are to be welcomed.

Public-private partnerships can play a major role, especially in urban areas and in telecommunications and energy. Project finance and a range of other private investment structures are being used in a growing number of developing countries to encourage private investment in infrastructure. The outcomes have been decidedly mixed. In the United Kingdom, which has a reasonably sophisticated policy environment, public–private partnerships have been found by the National Audit Office to provide poor value for money. In developing countries, following the bankruptcies of toll roads in Mexico and water utilities in Argentina, lessons have been learnt and developing countries now account for well over half of the private investments in infrastructure globally. Given infrastructure demands and the shortage of adequate government finance, there is a growing need for private power, telecommunications and other infrastructure investors to finance construction and operations. The mixed experience in recent decades points to the need for caution and the establishment of independent and powerful regulators to protect consumer interests from what can become natural monopolies or oligopolies.

Legal Framework and Equity

Laws serve to shape societies and, in particular, affect the nature of the relationships of citizens to each other and to their governments. Legal frameworks include the 'systems of rules and regulations, the norms that infuse them, and the means of adjudicating and enforcing them'. The rule of law has shaped development processes through the operation of laws, regulation and enforcement; enabled conditions and capacities necessary to development outcomes; and remained a core development end in itself. Therefore, the rule of law is of fundamental importance to development outcomes as it expresses and enables a society's conception of social and economic justice, and more specifically its attitudes to extreme poverty and deprivation. It also frames wealth, resource, and power (re)distribution.

An effective legal and judicial system is an essential component for economic development, as it is for human development and basic civil liberties. Ensuring that decision-making and justice are not determined by individual favours or corruption and that all citizens have equal access to the rule of law is vital to overcoming inequality and social exclusion. It is also required for the creation of transparent and well-functioning financial and other markets.

The relationship between the legal system and development is complex. In 1990, Douglas North and others pointed to a high positive correlation between the protection of property rights and long-term economic growth. Critics question whether the protection of property rights is a cause or a consequence of economic development. Similarly they question whether sound institutions are a cause or a consequence of development. In this respect several studies have shown that access to legal information and the rule of law can enhance participation and promote socio-economic development by empowering the poor and marginalized to claim rights, take advantage of economic and social opportunities and resist exploitation. The law and the courts can play an important role in defining identity and guaranteeing economic and social opportunities. The rule of law can improve access to service delivery by reallocating rights, privileges, duties, and powers. Strengthening legal institutions that prevent violence and crimes that undermine the well-being of citizens promotes development.

Legal institutions that promote accountability and transparency, and curb corruption can similarly facilitate development. Consistent and fair regulation and dispute resolution facilitates the smooth operation of the market system, and reduces the opportunities for corruption, nepotism, and rent seeking. The rule of law can also protect the environment and natural resources and promote sustainable development by enshrining workers', social, and environmental rights in constitutions and legislation.

Conflict, Peace, and Stability

Peace and stability, and the rule of law, are essential for development. War and conflict reverses development, not only through death and destruction, but also debilitating development by destroying and degrading infrastructure, institutions, and social cohesion. Although the world has been spared a global conflict since the Second World War—perhaps because all sides recognize that it could lead to mutually assured destruction—civil wars and armed conflicts have continued to bedevil development (see Figure 5). Over the last two decades, all main measures of civil wars (numbers, battle-related deaths, and civilian deaths) decreased, even though there has been an increase in global battle related deaths since 2013, mostly due to the Syrian crisis. In 2014, forty armed conflicts were recorded (the most since 1999) of which eleven resulted in more than 1,000 fatalities. Since the end of the Cold War in 1989, the number of battle-related deaths has fluctuated between 15,000 and 80,000 per annum, although the total number of fatalities—including civilians, women, and children is estimated to be much higher.

The impact of some of the more intense and enduring armed conflicts are reflected in life expectancy figures. In Sierra Leone, an eleven-year-long conflict reduced life expectancy to the mid-30s in the 1990s. In Nigeria, ongoing sectarian violence since the end of the civil war, along with the conflict in the Delta Niger, contributed to holding life expectancy at around forty-five years throughout the 1980s and 1990s. In the decade that followed, life expectancy has only managed to reach fifty-four years. Ongoing conflicts in Afghanistan, Syria, and Iraq have similarly affected life expectancy. Estimates of the number of fatalities in Syria from the start of the civil war in March 2011 to October

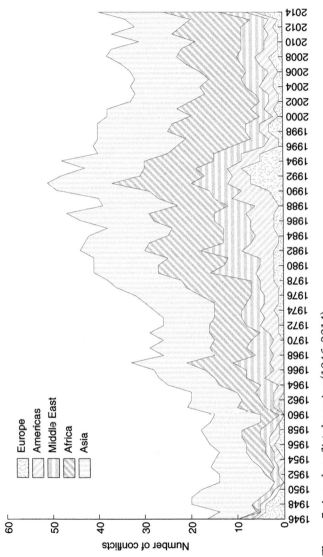

Figure 5 Armed conflicts by region (1946–2014).

2015 exceed 230,000, with the war cutting the average life expectancy in Syria by twenty years.

While conflict and war devastates lives and destroys development, peace and security are needed for economic and social development. Moreover, as the *World Development Report* of 2011 on 'Conflict, Security and Development' notes where development succeeds, countries become progressively safer from violent conflict, making subsequent development easier. However, where development fails, countries are at a high risk of becoming caught in a conflict trap in which war wrecks the economy and increases the risk of further war. *Fragile states* typically arise in post-conflict situations when the capacity of governments to manage is particularly weak. In these cases, capacity building is vital as is the engagement of civil society and non-governmental organizations (NGOs) which can provide much-needed organizational capabilities. The *World Development Report* showed that weak institutions trump a lack of growth as a cause of conflict, and that this is not only about low capacity institutions but unaccountable ones. Human rights abuses and corruption have a long-lasting legacy in causing later conflict, and the rule of law and justice underpins stability.

The relationship between political representation and peace has been the subject of numerous studies. Political development is thought to contribute to stability through the establishment of democratic institutions that ensure representation for all as well as checks and balances on executive power. Such views echo Immanuel Kant's influential pamphlet, *Perpetual Peace,* written in 1795. A number of modern studies confirm the statistical link.

Democratic states have, however, waged war against weaker states, as is evident in the United States interventions in Central America, Vietnam, Iraq, and elsewhere, France in Algeria, and the United Kingdom in Libya and Iraq. Democratic transitions may also contribute to ethnic violence. In some cases, such as the former Yugoslavia, the Caucasus, and Indonesia, transitions from dictatorship to more pluralistic political systems are associated with the rise of national independence movements, spurring separatist warfare that may spill over national borders. Newly independent states and 'anocracies' (unstable autocratic regimes with incoherent elements of democracy) are also particularly liable to fall into civil war. In this context, the collapse of South Sudan into civil war reflects a failure to adequately address the underlying grievances and the weakness of the governance structures that were erected to safeguard the fragile South Sudanese state.

Ethnicity and religious beliefs may have been key contributors to the conflict in the Balkans, as well as to conflicts in a number of African countries and the Middle East. However, these factors alone do not adequately explain eruptions of violence in which groups that co-existed for generations—as was the case with the Jews in Germany and Austria prior to the rise of Nazism, or Muslims in the Balkans and elsewhere—suddenly became the object of discrimination and brutal violence.

There are numerous national, regional, and global initiatives to reduce and prevent potential fault lines in society escalating into conflict. 'Light', 'direct', or 'operational' interventions attempt to prevent latent or threshold violence from becoming full-blown armed conflicts. Diplomatic interventions, United Nations missions and peace keeping forces are among the actions which can be invoked. Such measures do not usually address the root causes of conflict. Peacebuilding packages require a range of interventions, including post-war aid, provision of security, demilitarization, encouraging refugees to return, employment programmes, and other measures to revive the economy. Reforms of legal and political institutions, not least to guarantee human rights, may also be required. In addition to aid, the international community can apply political and economic pressure, resorting to economic sanctions, travel bans, and other actions against individuals, including possible arrest and transfer to the International Criminal Court in The Hague.

The United Nations is the primary international mechanism for conflict prevention. Its 1992 *Agenda for Peace* sets out comprehensive efforts to identify and support structures which will tend to consolidate peace and advance a sense of confidence and well-being among people. These include disarming the previously warring parties and the restoration of order, the custody and possible destruction of weapons, repatriating refugees, advisory and training support for security personnel, monitoring elections, advancing efforts to protect human rights, reforming or strengthening governmental institutions, and promoting formal and informal processes of political participation.

Under the United Nations Charter, the Security Council has primary responsibility for the maintenance of international peace and security. Its fifteen members—five of who are permanent and ten rotating on two-year terms—

are meant to determine the existence of a threat to peace or identify an act of international aggression. The Security Council has the authority to impose sanctions or authorize the use of force to restore peace. With Resolution 1366 of August 2001 the Security Council widened its mandate to include the Responsibility to Protect (R2P). This authorizes it to intervene in internal conflicts and prevent internal aggression or genocides within a country. In practice, because any of the permanent members—China, France, Russia, United Kingdom, and the United States—can veto any resolution, the Security Council has been unable to agree to take an active role in Syria or other recent conflicts. Even when it does, it depends on the actions of its members to implement its resolutions, severely limiting its ability to achieve the limited actions which have been agreed.

A number of initiatives in recent decades have sought to limit the financing of conflicts by restricting financial flows associated with investments in mining and other natural resources. The Extractive Industries Transparency Initiative aims to ensure that companies fully disclose the taxes and other payments made by oil, gas, and mining companies to governments. This aims to increase accountability and reduce the potential for the funds to be diverted for personal or political gain or for being used to buy arms and finance conflicts. The Kimberly Process is another example and is intended to stop the trade in 'conflict diamonds' which financed armaments. The process involves a global certification system designed to trace the origins of rough diamonds and to restrict trade outside certified channels. Another promising initiative is the International Arms Trade Treaty originally endorsed by the United Kingdom and Africa Commission in 2005. Despite slow progress through international institutions (such as the G8) and opposition from countries such as Cuba, Venezuela, and Egypt, the treaty entered into force in December 2014, having been ratified by sixty-one states.

5

⸺⸱∞∞∞⸱⸺

The Evolution of Development Aid

Foreign aid is any kind of *official development assistance* (ODA), concessionary loan, or financial grant given to developing countries mainly for the purpose of economic development or welfare provision. Table 4 shows that aid flows have increased in the post-war era. *Multilateral aid* is when aid is given by more than one state, typically through international institutions like the World Bank or United Nations. *Bilateral aid* is when one state—such as the United Kingdom, United States, France, or Germany—gives aid directly to another state. NGOs, such as the Gates Foundation, Oxfam, and Comic Relief have emerged as increasingly important donors of aid in the last two to three decades. What is new is the scale and reach of the contributions of non-state actors, rather than their recent arrival in the aid landscape; the Rockefeller Foundation was established in 1913, the Ford Foundation in 1936, and Oxfam in 1942.

Table 4. Average annual net aid flows received (1960–2014)

(Constant 2013 US$ millions)	1960–9	1970–9	1980–9	1990–9	2000–9	2010–14
Africa	11,808	19,367	29,568	31,853	39,051	52,611
North & Central America	1,378	2,040	4,179	4,223	4,002	5,353
South America	3,506	2,689	2,650	3,325	3,651	3,950
Middle East	1,983	7,944	9,170	5,472	12,188	14,391
South & Central Asia	10,148	10,439	11,964	9,307	13,171	19,345
Far East Asia	6,584	7,547	7,566	9,851	8,551	6,281
Europe	2,615	1,205	1,448	3,561	5,613	7,846
Oceania	934	2,384	2,742	2,545	1,566	2,064

Source: Author's calculation based on OECD, https://stats.oecd.org/qwids/ (last accessed 7 February 2016).

The term aid covers a wide variety of interventions. Aid can include technical assistance, infrastructure projects, structural adjustment measures, political objectives, education and welfare programmes, humanitarian work, disaster relief, and even medical aid or programmes to eliminate the production of drugs—the programmes administered by the United States to eradicate coca plants in Colombia are classed as aid as are the equivalent programmes to destroy opiate poppy cultivation in Afghanistan. Examples of humanitarian work and disaster relief include food aid and vaccination programmes. Vaccination programmes have had a dramatic impact, as evidenced by the elimination of smallpox and the curtailment of many other endemic diseases.

Aid has at times contributed greatly to development, but has also, at times, undermined development. Much harm was done during the Cold War, when aid was used as a political and military tool, to advance geo-political goals rather than to achieve development objectives. Not surprisingly, aid was wasted and counterproductive when given to governments that used it for purposes other than to reduce poverty, and when it went to corrupt politicians or to support expensive high maintenance and ineffective 'white elephant' projects, which often were tied to the use of the donors' experts and export businesses. There are numerous historical examples of such abuses, including the transfer of over $10 billion (£6.5 billion) to Mobutu, the former dictator of Zaire (known today as the Democratic Republic of the Congo). However, to condemn all aid as a result of past failures is inappropriate, as these failures never characterized most aid, and increasingly they represent exceptions in a much-improved aid landscape.

Since the end of the Cold War the effectiveness of aid has increased. More than sixty developing countries have become democratic in Africa, Latin America, and Asia, and macroeconomic management has improved in most recipient countries. There is also greater transparency and scrutiny in recipient countries. Donors have become more coordinated. The MDGs and alignment of donors has provided common direction. The OECD Development Assistance Committee (DAC) has helped through peer review and collective scrutiny to engender a more coordinated approach and to reduce abuse. The OECD DAC no longer includes military aid as development assistance and has reduced the abuse of export credits and other tied flows. Tied aid was commonplace until the 1990s, and included the requirement that aid be used for payments in the donor country, or in a group of specified countries, typically to pay for machinery, consultants, and other products and services from the country providing the aid. Firms exporting to developing countries could also benefit from export credits by which aid was used to provide concessional financing, in the forms of loans, insurance, and guarantees.

As the conceptual understanding of development has advanced, donors and recipients have become better at identifying what works and what does not, including for example through the introduction of techniques such as randomized trials. Developing countries' expertise has also improved and the dependency of recipients on the international donors and experts who previously monopolized aid has been reduced with the growth of capital markets and rise of new bilateral donors, such as China and India. For these interrelated reasons, the overall effectiveness of aid is now greater than at any point in history and continues to improve.

Studies by David Dollar and others found that in 1990 countries with the worst policies received more per capita in terms of ODA than countries with better policies ($44 as opposed to $39); by the late 1990s the situation was reversed: those with better policies received almost twice as much in per capita terms ($28 versus $16). As a result the poverty reduction effectiveness per dollar of overall ODA has grown rapidly.

Changing Aid

International aid emerged as a phenomenon after the Second World War, and has its origins in The European Recovery Programme—or Marshall Plan—which funded post-war reconstruction in Europe and parts of Asia as well as British, French, and other colonial territories. Early theories of development emphasized the need for interventions by governments in poor countries to exercise a decisive role in investment and industrialization. As noted earlier in this volume, development planners advocated a big push for industrial development to help overcome bottlenecks in savings and investment markets and to provide vital infrastructure. Modernization theorists argued that developing countries merely lacked the finance required to fuel a take-off into self-sustained growth.

Initially aid focused on supporting former colonies or was distributed for political or military reasons connected with the Cold War. But by the 1970s international aid agencies began to focus on growth, income distribution, and also increasingly on basic needs. Since 1990, the end of the Cold War has allowed for greater aid effectiveness by targeting poverty reduction efforts more directly.

In 2000, the MDGs, for the first time, established clearly identified and measurable shared objectives for the 189 national signatories. At a series of subsequent meetings donors committed to align themselves behind national development programmes. The 2005 Paris Declaration on Aid Effectiveness emphasized the commitment of the recipient countries to the success of the aid-funded projects (which became known as 'ownership'), alignment of donors' policies, a focus on results and outcomes, and mutual accountability between donors and recipients. The 2008 Accra Agenda for Action reaffirmed the importance of strengthening country ownership, building effective partnerships, and development outcomes as did the subsequent 2011 Aid Effectiveness Summit in Busan, South Korea. In July 2015 a United Nations Conference on Financing for Development held in Addis Ababa, Ethiopia reviewed the progress made in previous conferences and sought to address the new and emerging issues articulated in the SDGs, including the financing of investments required to address climate change.

Total ODA is now around $149 billion (£95 billion), representing a 69 per cent increase in real terms since the MDGs were agreed in 2000. Most aid goes to middle-income countries and strategically important countries, such as

Colombia, Egypt and more recently Afghanistan and Iraq have received large amounts of aid which is not allocated on the basis of the concentration of poverty in these countries, but rather instability and conflict.

ODA, as proportion of donor countries' GNI, has declined from about 0.35 per cent in the late 1960s to around 0.29 per cent in 2015. A United Nations resolution in October 1970 had committed the advanced countries to a target of allocating 0.7 per cent of their national income to foreign aid by 1975, a target that only Sweden met. In 1970 the OECD DAC members also agreed that they would commit 0.7 per cent of their national income to development. Subsequently this target has been reaffirmed repeatedly, including at the 2005 G8 Gleneagles Summit and the 2005 United Nations World Summit. Forty years after its original agreement, in addition to Sweden only four of the twenty-eight other DAC members have met the target—Denmark, Luxembourg, Norway, and the United Kingdom, which is the only one of the G7 members to have enshrined this commitment into law.

Aid flows typically make up a small part of the budget of developing countries—on average well under 2 per cent, although for the poorest countries this can exceed 10 per cent. For particular countries at particular times these flows can play a vital role in addressing budget shortfalls or shocks, such as those that arise from a natural disaster or collapse in commodity prices.

Not surprisingly, good institutions and sound public policy increase the effectiveness of aid. Even well-designed projects can be undermined by macroeconomic instability or corruption. Weak local institutions and the domination of foreign donors can lead to failures in the implementation of a policy or programme. Local ownership and the commitment of national and community leaders to projects are vital for aid effectiveness.

Millennium and Sustainable Development Goals

The Millennium Development Goals emerged through high-level negotiations in policy circles, drawing on international agreements reached over the previous decades. The United Nations' MDGs go beyond the DAC targets and represent a major step forward in many respects (see Box 3). For the first time in the history of development, a global partnership was established with an alignment of donors' and the recipients' aims and instruments, and the establishment of agreed goals, targets, and indicators. While there was much debate about the selection of the eight

---

BOX 3   *Millennium Development Goals*

Goal 1: Eradicate extreme poverty and hunger

Goal 2: Achieve universal primary education

Goal 3: Promote gender equality and empower women

Goal 4: Reduce child mortality

Goal 5: Improve maternal health

Goal 6: Combat HIV/AIDS, malaria, and other diseases

Goal 7: Ensure environmental sustainability

Goal 8: Develop a global partnership for development

---

goals, and definition and measurement of the twenty-one targets and sixty intermediate indicators, the establishment of a common and transparent framework was a major achievement.

Progress towards the achievement of the MDGs over its fifteen-year horizon has been uneven. The first target of halving world poverty has been achieved, with the number of people living in extreme poverty falling by just over one billion (compared to the 1990 base), thanks largely to the great strides made by China, primarily with its own resources (see Figure 12). For most countries, however, progress has fallen short on the first goal and many of the other MDGs, while for many of the poorest African countries the data simply does not exist to assess achievements.

In September 2015, at the largest ever gathering of heads of state in New York, a new set of SDGs were agreed (Box 4). The SDGs, like the MDGs, reflect the evolving state of development thinking. Unlike the MDGs, which were widely perceived to be a top-down exercise cooked up by diplomats and technocrats at the United Nations and OECD, the United Nations established an Open Working Group to develop the new goals. The growing range and power of articulate and organized stakeholders has widened participation in the development agenda. The growing evidence of new challenges to development, not least those arising from climate change and the threat to ecological systems, has also widened the range of development concerns. The SDGs have seventeen goals with 169 targets covering a broad range of sustainable development issues, including ending poverty and hunger, improving health and education,

BOX 4 *Sustainable Development Goals*

··

Goal 1: End poverty in all its forms everywhere

Goal 2: End hunger, achieve food security and improved nutrition, and promote sustainable agriculture

Goal 3: Ensure healthy lives and promote well-being for all at all ages

Goal 4: Ensure inclusive and quality education for all and promote lifelong learning

Goal 5: Achieve gender equality and empower all women and girls

Goal 6: Ensure access to water and sanitation for all

Goal 7: Ensure access to affordable, reliable, sustainable, and modern energy for all

Goal 8: Promote inclusive and sustainable economic growth, employment, and decent work for all

Goal 9: Build resilient infrastructure, promote sustainable industrialization, and foster innovation

Goal 10: Reduce inequality within and among countries

Goal 11: Make cities inclusive, safe, resilient, and sustainable

Goal 12: Ensure sustainable consumption and production patterns

Goal 13: Take urgent action to combat climate change and its impacts

Goal 14: Conserve and sustainably use the oceans, seas, and marine resources

Goal 15: Sustainably manage forests, combat desertification, halt and reverse land degradation, halt biodiversity loss

Goal 16: Promote just, peaceful, and inclusive societies

Goal 17: Revitalize the global partnership for sustainable development making cities more sustainable, combating climate change, and protecting oceans and forests. These goals and targets will be further elaborated through the creation of hundreds of indicators focused on measurable outcomes.

The SDGs go beyond the MDGs to incorporate a wider range of issues and actors. This reflects the growing recognition that there is no silver bullet for development and that beyond markets and the state, the role of cities, new donors, businesses, and natural systems must be incorporated into development agendas. This more nuanced approach to development is welcome, but it brings new challenges, including adding a greater burden of management, measurement and coordination to an already overstretched and at times overwhelmingly complex understanding of how development happens and how it may be measured.

Development Finance Institutions

Development finance institutions (DFIs) operate at the global, regional, and national level to provide finance, technical support, and other services to promote development. These institutions tend to draw on public funds—taxpayers' money. They leverage the commitment of governments to underwrite their lending to raise further funds at lower costs than capital markets are able to provide. The aim is then to pass on the benefits of this lower cost of funding to developing countries. When supported by more than one government, the DFIs are also known as multilateral development banks (MDBs) or international financial institutions (IFIs).

The International Bank for Reconstruction and Development (IBRD) was established at the Bretton Woods Conference in 1945 to assist with the reconstruction of Europe and Japan following the devastation of the Second World War. The IBRD has leveraged the $14 billion of capital paid in by its 188 members to create $360 billion of loans. The IBRD is part of the World Bank group, which has assets exceeding $550 billion and includes the International Development Agency (IDA) which provides highly concessional loans to the poorest countries, the Multilateral Investment Guarantee Agency (MIGA) which sells political risk guarantees to investors, and the International Finance Corporation (IFC), which invests in the private sector in developing countries. The IFC is the largest of the specialist development institutions which facilitates private capital flows into developing countries. Since its establishment in 1956 it has invested over $50 billion in more than a hundred countries.

The DFIs are subject to the political preferences of their dominant shareholders, which in the case of the World Bank are the G7 powers. They also are influenced by academic and policy perceptions. Policy changed in the 1990s when a new strand of scholarly work emerged that highlighted the importance of institutions, led by Nobel Prize winners Ronald Coase, Douglas North, and Joseph Stiglitz, and Stiglitz was appointed Chief Economist of the World Bank in 1997 under James Wolfensohn. In 1999, reflecting a more heterodox approach to development than had previously prevailed, the World Bank adopted a Comprehensive Development Framework (CDF) which sought to advance a holistic approach to development that balances macroeconomic with structural, human and physical development needs. The CDF was made operational through Poverty Reduction Strategy Papers (PRSPs) focusing on the priorities for reforms and investments in individual recipient countries where country ownership was said to be vital. However, the link between CDF and PRSPs was uneven, and as the World Bank decentralized in response to a perceived need for activities to be more responsive to country needs, the unevenness in its application became more pronounced, with the weight placed on different dimensions of the CDF varying according to the interplay of the decentralized Bank leaders and their national counterparts.

Meanwhile, at the United Nations Development Programme (UNDP), the *Human Development Approach* went beyond economic indicators to place broader measures of the well-being of people at the centre of development concerns. As the UNDP's resources and capabilities were much smaller than those of the World Bank and other multilateral banks, its influence was mainly in the realm of ideas.

Following the establishment of the World Bank, the international community established the Inter-American Development Bank (1959), African Development Bank (1963) and Asian Development Bank (1966) and more recently, following the collapse of the Soviet Union, the European Bank for Reconstruction and Development (1991).

Publicly owned development banks have also been established at the sub-regional level. The largest of these is the European Investment Bank (EIB), which is owned by the European Union member countries. The EIB supports the development of infrastructure and other assets in European countries and developing countries that have relations with the European Union and has assets exceeding €500 billion. Other sub-regions have similarly established development banks. These include the Development Bank of Southern Africa (DBSA) where I was Chief Executive. Following the end of apartheid the DBSA became the largest funder of infrastructure in the fourteen countries of the southern Africa region. Similar institutions include the Corporación Andina de Fomento (CAF)—covering Andean countries—the Caribbean Development Bank and in 2015 the addition of two major new initiatives, the New Development Bank—established by Brazil, Russia, India, China, and South Africa (the BRICS)—and the Chinese-inspired Asian Infrastructure Investment Bank.

National development banks have a longer history than the multilateral institutions. KfW (whose name originally comes from Kreditanstalt für Wiederaufbau—the 'Reconstruction Credit Institute') was established in 1948 to assist with the reconstruction of Germany and played a major role in the reunification of East and West Germany in the 1990s and is also an agency for German development investments abroad. Subsequently, many advanced and developing countries have established development banks. The extent to which they continue to play a positive role depends on their ability to reform in light of the changing circumstances.

The development of active private sector capital markets and decline in ideas of import substitution protectionism, which protected selected industries and firms from imports and domestic competition, has removed the primary purpose of many industrial development banks. These state banks typically financed protected firms, at subsidized interest rates. Where they have undertaken necessary reforms, national development banks can, however, continue to have a vital role to play in fostering infrastructure and small business development in areas where there is market failure. The establishment in 2012 by the Conservative government in the United Kingdom of the Green Investment Bank to use public funds to leverage private investment in renewal technologies is a modern adaption of development banking. The largest national development banks are in China. The China Development Bank has assets of over $1.2 trillion, well over double those of the World Bank group. While most of its lending is within China, its annual lending to developing countries now exceeds that of the World Bank.

In addition to providing development aid, a number of countries have national DFIs that invest in developing countries through a combination of grants, loans, and private equity investments. The biggest bilateral donors are the United States, which has a core budget of around $10 billion and in the United Kingdom, the Department for International Development (DFID) which has an annual budget of over £11 billion ($17 billion) that is scheduled to grow to over £16 billion by 2020. DFID is the sole shareholder of the CDC Group (CDC, formerly the Commonwealth Development Corporation) which invests to support private sector investment in poor developing countries. (I have been the senior independent non-executive director on the CDC board since 1996.) Similarly, the Agence Française de Développement (AFD) and its private sector agency Proparco, the German KfW development agency and its private sector affiliate DEG, the Dutch Development Bank FMO, and the Japan International Cooperation Agency (JICA) are among the many examples of national development institutions focusing on the development of both public and private sectors.

DFIs contribute significantly to development. When following best practice, they add to the capacity of the recipient governments to build infrastructure, education, health, and other foundations for development, as well as contributing to the development of the private sector.

Effective development support requires that the many lessons of past failures be learnt and that the agencies coordinate and harmonize their policies to ensure that they do not add to the burden of administration and subvert national decision-making. As economies grow and the capacity of governments to raise taxes and investment increases, along with the savings of individuals and the development of capital markets, the role of DFIs also needs to change. As governments' budgetary capacity and capital markets develop, the comparative advantage of development agencies increasingly is in the area of public goods, where the market is unable to provide much-needed investments. For poor countries, this includes public infrastructure, health, education, and other systems that governments cannot afford to invest in adequately.

In addition to supplementing national government's ability to finance the 'hardware' of development, the international institutions have an important role to play in both poor and middle-income countries in sharing ideas and lessons learnt from comparative experience, to assist in the building of the 'software' of development. This includes legal and regulatory systems which foster open and transparent societies that increase the voice of citizens and reduce what economists call 'rent seeking', which leads to the perversion of development by small groups of beneficiaries through protectionism, monopolist practices, or corruption.

DFIs can also play a catalytic role in the mobilization of domestic and foreign savings to support private sector development, with institutions such as the IFC, CDC, Proparco, and others investing alongside the private sector to reduce risk and provide what the European Bank of Reconstruction and Development (EBRD) calls 'additionality' to encourage private investments that may not otherwise have occurred. The financial support provided by DFIs is small compared to the finance mobilized by commercial banks and private equity groups. Nevertheless, in 'frontier' markets the particularly tough working environment and small scale of operations typically means that the private sector is unwilling to provide the longer-term finance required for power generation and other infrastructure. With just one of the larger commercial banks, which have individual assets exceeding $2 trillion, far exceeding the potential to mobilize funding of the international DFIs, it is the development finance focus and the unique knowledge and relations that the DFIs bring, which differentiates them. Where DFIs provide finance and skills which supplement official flows by financing projects that the private sector will not finance, and they leverage and encourage private finance, rather than compete with private sources, they will continue to have a significant role in the future.

Debt Crisis and Response

As noted earlier, in the 1970s, many African, Latin American, and South Asian countries borrowed extensively to finance their big push for industrialization (Figure 6). With the oil price shocks of the late 1970s and the global recession in the early 1980s, the current accounts (balance of trade and other exports over imports) and capital accounts (financial inflows versus capital outflows) of many developing countries went into deficit. A growing number of developing countries became dependent on large flows of aid to finance their foreign imports and the interest payments on their debt. The resulting debt crisis resulted from growing imbalances between finance flowing out (or owed) and inward flows. Between 1985 and 1988 the average outflow from the world's poor countries to advanced economies, was $11 billion each year. By the mid 1990s the crisis had worsened, so that for every $1 given in aid, $9 was taken back through debt repayments.

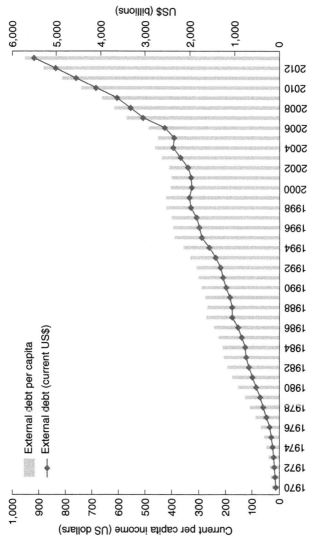

Figure 6 External debt of developing countries (1970–2013).

The outflow of finance to repay debt compounded the failure of many countries to mobilize sufficient savings domestically to meet their investment needs. The availability of domestic resources to finance development has been further undermined by individuals and firms sending their personal funds (and those they have misappropriated from the state and others through corrupt practices) elsewhere, often to secretive tax havens. This *capital flight* has been very significant in Latin America and Africa, and for Africa alone is estimated to exceed one trillion dollars since 1970. Capital flight is associated with the illegal or illicit transfer of funds abroad, which means it does not appear in recorded national statistics and can only be estimated. A major source of capital flight involves the under-invoicing of exports and over-invoicing of imports, with the trade partner depositing the difference in a foreign account. Resource-rich countries with poor governance suffer from the highest levels of capital flight, relative to the size of their economies, but the size of the elite and economy also matters, which is why Brazil and South Africa, and more recently China and India, are thought to be among the largest sources of capital flight.

Following the debt crisis, private sources of finance dried up, and donors empowered the IMF and World Bank, in which they exercised a decisive influence due to the shareholding arrangements, to restore stability and ensure repayment of foreign debt. The IMF and World Bank exercised an effective monopoly on finance and as a result were able to dictate the conditions of the bailouts and the terms of the reintegration of the developing countries into global capital markets. Without the agreement of the Fund, no private bank or

OECD donor would provide support to the heavily indebted countries. The impact of the concentration of absolute power in the Fund, in coordination with the World Bank, as well as their inequitable governance structure, continues to generate resentment to this day.

The Fund and Bank coordinated their programmes closely, with the Fund offering the prospect of short-term balance of payments support, and the Bank long-term loans, as long as a set of conditions, which became known as structural adjustment programmes were met. The conditions which were sequenced to coincide with the releases of tranches of funds included the liberalization of exchange rates, the restoration of fiscal and trade balances, the privatization of state-owned enterprises, and sharp reductions in expenditure and in the money supply to reduce fiscal deficits and to limit inflation to low single digits. For many countries the resulting contractionary impact was severe and deeply unpopular, with numerous governments losing power.

The extremely painful consequence of the debt crisis led many developing countries to vow to never again to have to return to the IMF and World Bank cap in hand in positions of desperation. The resulting macroeconomic orthodoxy has become etched into the political economy of most developing countries. Exceptions, such as Venezuela and Argentina, are now the outliers.

In an irony of history, the advanced economies that preached macroeconomic orthodoxy failed to follow their own advice. The result is that the United States, Japan, the United Kingdom, and indeed virtually all other advanced economies are in poor economic shape, with levels of debt approximately similar to that of many of the developing countries in the 1970s and 1980s. Structural adjustment programmes have been shown to be ill conceived in that they undermined key foundations of development and reduced the potential for escaping the cycle of debt crisis. Excessive cuts to health, education, research, and infrastructure systems undermined the growth potential. The danger is that the terrible lessons of the previous epoch of debt crises have not been learnt, and that Greece and other countries are condemned to repeat the experience of many developing countries as they seek to escape the spiral of debt.

Since the late 1990s, the majority of developing countries have restored their national finances and are now far less indebted than the advanced economies. International aid has significantly contributed to this improvement. The creation of the Heavily Indebted Poor Countries (HIPC) initiative in 1996 provided relief for thirty-nine countries suffering from unsustainable debt. In 2005 the *Make Poverty History* campaign and the G8 summit at Gleneagles Scotland allocated a further $40 billion to debt relief. In 2006 the HIPC programme was supplemented with the Multilateral Debt Relief Initiative, which allowed for full relief of debt in eligible low income countries to free up resources for poverty reduction.

International Public Goods

Directed aid from bilateral or multilateral donors can play a highly significant role in assisting individual countries in achieving their development ambitions. The role of the international community in creating the conditions conducive for development and in supporting the creation of international public goods is even more important.

Global public goods are goods that have an impact which goes beyond any one country. These goods are not generally provided by the market due to their non-excludable and non-rival nature. That is, individuals cannot be excluded from consuming them, and one person's enjoyment of these goods does not diminish the consumption of others. Furthermore, global public goods cannot be monopolized for the benefit of any one country. Notable examples include financial stability, global human security (peace), the global commons (clean air, rain forests, oceans), and public health (including tackling infectious diseases such as smallpox, malaria, or river blindness). In addition to these, an equitable global trading system, the prevention of climate change and the creation of new vaccines or rice strains may be added to the list of global public goods.

The common characteristics of these goods are that their benefits spill over national borders and that they cannot be created by the private sector alone. Global public goods are increasingly becoming an important part of the development agenda. Even if poverty is eradicated and in the future no individual countries require development assistance, the international community is likely to have an increasing role to play in financing and supporting the provision of cross-border public goods.

Past examples of innovative global programmes that underline the benefit of economic aid being directed to multi-country or global programmes include the Onchocerciasis Control Programme, established in 1974, to tackle river blindness in West Africa. This disease caused blindness, disfigurement, and unbearable itching in its victims and rendered tracts of farmland uninhabitable. The eradication programme halted transmission and virtually eliminated the prevalence of onchocerciasis throughout the eleven-country sub-region containing 35 million people. The wide-ranging benefits of this achievement included the prevention of 600,000 cases of blindness, sparing 18 million children from the risk of river blindness, and the establishment of 25 million hectares of land which was safe for cultivation and resettlement.

More recently, rates of death from malaria have plunged by 60 per cent in the period 2000 to 2015, and new cases of the parasitic mosquito-borne disease declined by 37 per cent over this fifteen-year period as a result of the success of the global Roll Back Malaria initiative, which focuses on providing access to insecticide-treated mosquito nets, diagnostic testing, and Artemisinin-based therapies, as well as spraying and associated activities. The decline has been associated with nineteen countries being on the verge of eliminating the disease. Despite this progress, malaria remains a devastating threat to development, resulting in an estimated 215 million people becoming infected each year of which over 430,000 still die each year, highlighting the extent to which further actions are needed.

Another example of the impact of global aid programmes is the CGIAR consortium which was associated with the Green Revolution in the 1970s. The development of high yield crops led to impressive gains in food output and lower food prices for the poor. As a result of investments by the international community, coupled with capacity building in many countries, the yields of cereals and coarse grain more than doubled in Asia and Latin America. A key development challenge today is to extend this green revolution to Africa and ensure that productivity increases can continue in the face of climate and other major challenges to sustainability.

Public goods which are supported by development aid may also be in the realm of the advancement of skills and ideas. An example of this is the African Economic Research Consortium (AERC), which was established in 1988 to strengthen local capacity for conducting independent, rigorous inquiry into problems pertinent to the management of economies in sub-Saharan Africa. The AERC supports researchers and academic institutions, as well as various MA programmes in economics. By enabling local policy analysis and formulation it provides a public good for African economies.

Building Resilience

Stopping global catastrophes requires much higher levels of investment in global public goods. It is easy to show how the risks in any one country can spill over national borders and have dramatic consequences elsewhere. A pandemic starting in any poor country, or a fundamentalist movement gaining ground in a failed state, poses a potential threat to even the richest and most advanced countries.

Investing in international health, peace, and development is therefore in all of our interests.

Risks do not only arise in poor countries, but poor people and poor countries are most vulnerable to risk. This is both because they do not have the savings, insurance, and other means to protect themselves from risks (for example by investing in flood defences, irrigation, or robust infrastructure), and because the poorest tend to be concentrated in the most risky places—such as slums without sanitation and on fragile agricultural lands which are vulnerable to flooding and valley floors and floodplains which are prone to flooding.

Climate change poses a major challenge to all countries. It exacerbates poverty and has potentially devastating consequences for communities vulnerable to the rise of ocean levels or a climate shock to agricultural systems. Scientists are in no doubt that the problem has arisen due to cumulative greenhouse gas emissions, and particularly the atmospheric absorption of carbon dioxide, from the increased burning of fossil fuels over the past two hundred years since industrialization began.

While the progress of currently rich countries has been inextricably linked to their use of fossil fuels, the slowing of climate change requires that the future flow of emissions be severely curtailed. As developing countries now account for more than half of emissions, the question of how they can climb the energy ladder and provide much-needed energy to meet their electricity, transport, and other energy demands without compounding the impact of climate change is an extraordinarily difficult development challenge. The resolution of this challenge cannot fall on the shoulders of the developing countries alone and for economic, political, and ethical reasons requires that the rich countries shoulder a significant part of the burden. As the slowing of climate change becomes an essential international public good, the rapid transfer of game-changing flows of finance—estimated at well over $100 billion per year—is required. This needs to be accompanied by the facilitation of technological transfers and provision of expertise to help developing countries increase their energy consumption, while slowing—and in the not-too-distant future stopping—their carbon and other greenhouse gas emissions.

The scale of these required transfers points to the transformation of the nature, purpose, and destination of aid flows, but not to their decline.

The Future of Aid

Aid flows have never been more effective in encouraging growth and reducing poverty. The reasons are simple. Firstly, developing countries have never been better governed, and their economies have never been more effectively managed. Secondly, aid is increasingly flowing to those countries which are able to use it effectively, rather than being directed by Cold War, military, or other geostrategic objectives. Thirdly, the aid community and academia have evolved over the past seventy years. There is a better understanding of what works and what does not and of the need for coherence between aid and macroeconomic, trade, and other policies. Significantly, common processes, and goalposts have been established. These are articulated most forcefully in the MDGs and reaffirmed in the SDGs, which have greatly improved the effectiveness of aid and reduced tied aid, vanity projects, and corruption.

The experience of development assistance since the Second World War provides for a large range of experiences from which to draw lessons. Aid still is given for military and strategic purposes, for example, to Afghanistan and Egypt, for international security purposes, and to projects directed at the eradication of drugs in Colombia. But as the number of countries needing aid has reduced, and the number of government and non-government donors has grown, the potential for making a real difference where it matters is greater than ever. This is the case both at the country level and in supporting international public goods.

With over half of the world's poor now living in what the World Bank defines as middle-income countries, including China and Brazil, a key question for the international community is the extent to which these countries require external financial or technical assistance to achieve their development objectives. China has $3.5 trillion in reserves and for a country like Brazil, aid flows are a tiny fraction—well under 1 per cent—of budgeted expenditures.

The international community can nevertheless continue to make a significant difference in a wide variety of ways in middle-income countries as well as in poor countries. Actions also need to be taken to benefit all countries through supporting international public goods, including through securing a resolution of the Doha Development Round of trade negotiations and effective climate change and other agreements, as well as support for the CGIAR, public health, and other public goods. Even in middle-income countries, the international community can make a major difference by investing in projects and programmes where the potential *demonstration effect* is large. As aid is typically small in relation to the financing needs, the ability to *scale* up and learn lessons from aid-financed projects is a key criterion of success for development interventions. Leverage should be sought both in development lessons learnt and in terms of finance, in that the success of the project leads to further investments from official and private funds. The DFIs have a particular role to play in furthering best practice and maximizing the demonstration effect of their projects.

The World Bank has the greatest potential due to the breadth and depth of its experience, the scale of its operations, and its internal capacity. It, however, has failed to draw sufficiently on the lessons of its seventy-five-year history of development and its global perspectives to share insights into what works and does not work. The World Bank has the potential to contribute more significantly by becoming an effective global knowledge bank on development and a financier of global public goods. Such a sharing of lessons can be particularly valuable in solving the seemingly toughest development challenges, such as those of particular countries and regions which face intractable poverty and in fragile states.

As more and more countries escape poverty, it is possible to envisage a rapidly reducing requirement for international development assistance and for this to be concentrated on the poorest and most fragile states, post-conflict and humanitarian aid, and disaster recovery. There also is a growing role for engagement in international public goods.

Middle-income countries have benefited greatly from private financial flows, with direct foreign investment, private equity, debt, and remittances far exceeding aid flows to these countries (see Figure 7). However, private financial flows have not benefited the majority of least developed countries, as the flows have been directed principally to extractive industries in a handful of the poorest countries, leaving them highly dependent on aid and, increasingly, on remittances.

Since the 1990s private sector investment (including foreign investment) has become the principal source of finance for development for middle-income developing countries. For developing countries as a whole, foreign direct investment flows exceed global ODA flows by a factor of at least four in recent years (see Figure 8). Private equity flows—in which foreigners invest in funds which buy direct stakes in businesses in developing countries—have increased rapidly, with over $3 billion in private equity allocated for investment in a very wide range of African countries in the first six months of 2015 alone. Encouraging responsible private investment, not least in the countries where capital is lacking, requires the establishment of national and international rules, regulations, and norms. Institutions like the IFC and CDC, which are dedicated to development and are able to mobilize patient capital and identify opportunities for private investment in even the toughest environments, have a vital role to play in this regard.

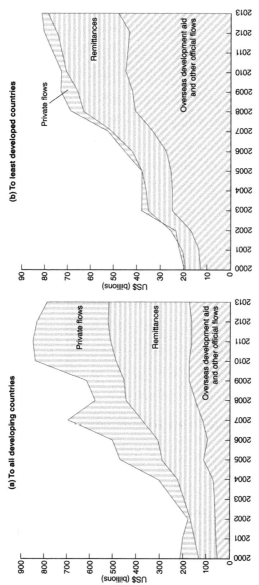

Figure 7 Financial flows to developing and least developed countries (2000–13).

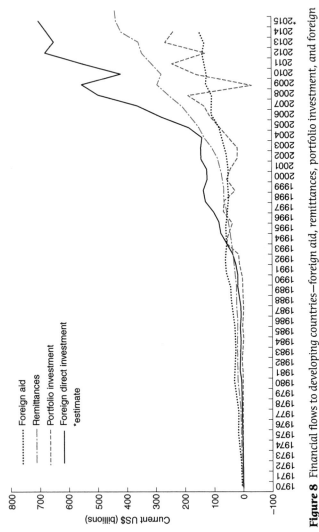

Figure 8 Financial flows to developing countries—foreign aid, remittances, portfolio investment, and foreign direct investment (1970–2015).

Creating pools of 'development capital' which may be used to underpin pioneering investments in developing countries provides an additional instrument in development agencies' toolkit. The use of public funds to leverage private sector investment can take many forms, including co-financing, guarantees, subordinated loans (in which the private investors would be repaid first in the event of default), and co-investments, in which the public sector investors may accept returns which are lower than the higher profits anticipated by private investors.

Innovative finance mechanisms encompass a widening range of financial instruments, and often involve a partnership between the public and private sectors. Innovative financial partnerships are estimated to have grown by 11 per cent per year since 2001, and to have mobilized well over $100 billion. Much of this growth can be attributed to the emergence of new financing instruments. Among the products are green and other thematic bonds, guarantees, performance-based contracts, impact-investing funds, advanced market commitments, debt-swaps, and development impact bonds.

It has been estimated that the SDGs will require approximately $2.5 trillion per year, which is over double the current public and private investment in the countries concerned. To this must be added the urgent investments required to reduce carbon emissions, while still allowing developing countries to overcome their often-crippling energy deficits. The implication is that much higher levels of aid (particularly for the least developed countries) and of private finance (for all developing countries) are required.

Figure 9 and Figure 10 show that the origin as well as the composition and volume of international aid have evolved in recent years. Aid flows between developing countries are becoming more significant. The OECD estimated that in 2013 China gave over $3 billion, Saudi Arabia over $5.7 billion, and India and Brazil over $1 billion each. China's relationship with Africa has received widespread attention. This relationship has a long history, with the Tanzam 1,860 kilometre (1,160 mile) long railway having been constructed between Tanzania and Zambia with Chinese finance and support in the 1970s. In recent years, extensive Chinese investment has been associated with Chinese reintegration

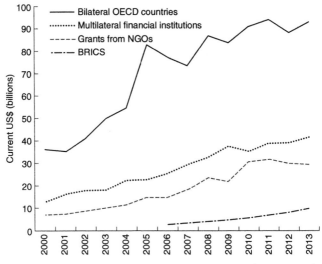

Figure 9 Traditional and non-traditional aid donors (2000–2013).

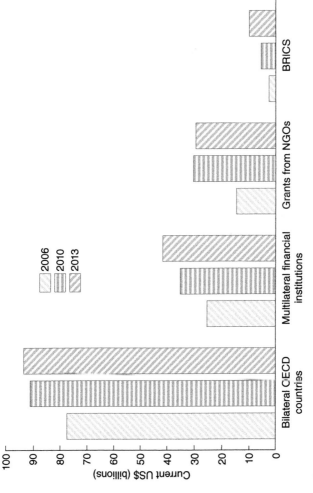

Figure 10 The rise of non-traditional aid donors.

into the world economy, including through the purchase of significant shareholdings in firms based in developing countries.

From a development perspective, the diversification of sources of finance and ideas is welcome even though the terms of engagement and the extent to which they are harmonized with those established by the Development Assistance Committee (DAC) of the OECD group of rich countries remains to be resolved. OECD donors in recent years have committed to reduce support for dictators and to limit corruption, and it is important that the new donors do not provide a backdoor to the financing of corrupt and autocratic regimes.

Aid from private foundations and philanthropists has also grown. In addition to the proliferation of private giving, organizations such as Band Aid and Comic Relief with campaigns such as Make Poverty History have captured the hearts and minds of the public. Through its Red Nose Day and Sports Relief activities, Comic Relief has raised cumulatively over a billion pounds, allowing it to contribute to the education of over one million children in Africa, buy bed nets which protect over 6 million people from malaria in Africa, and also connect with development challenges in the United Kingdom, for example by establishing a domestic violence helpline for women and children which has taken over 1.5 million calls.

The latest estimates are that at around $60 billion per annum, total private giving is about half of total official aid flows which are at about $135 billion per annum. The largest single private donor is the Gates Foundation, which in 2014 donated $4 billion out of its foundation funds of around $41.3 billion.

The key question for philanthropic donations as for all financial and other flows is the extent to which they act as catalysts for development. Domestic savings and investment together with government finance in virtually all countries dwarf official and private international flows. The impact of international aid flows depends on the extent to which they provide a source of best practice, signal confidence in countries, and tackle the most difficult problems which may be neglected or insufficiently tackled by local sources.

Private finance is vital. It is the private sector that creates jobs and growth. Yet effective governments are necessary for development. Private flows should therefore not undermine effective government. In those cases where such flows support corruption, cronyism, or predatory elites, or if they are simply geared towards resource extraction and make use of offshore tax havens so that they do not contribute taxes to national exchequers, or if they divert scarce national skills and resources to vanity projects, they may well undermine development. Philanthropists can do immense good. However, if their agendas are not aligned with national priorities they can distort them. For example, certain evangelical groups have made the prevention of birth control a condition of their funding for communities, with negative economic consequences. As with ODA, the conditions attached to the flows are often at least as important as the flows themselves in shaping development outcomes.

Evaluation

The extent to which aid will matter in the longer term depends on how it might lead to broader systemic changes and whether it leverages in additional flows of domestic and foreign investment. For aid to have a catalytic effect, it needs to be scaled up so that its positive impact is felt well beyond the confines of the original project. To judge whether this is the case, development impact and outcomes have to be assessed. However, evaluation typically has been undertaken by the donors and international agencies as a form of audit of their past activities and has rarely informed future activities. It has not provided timely feedback which may inform mid-course corrections or improvements to existing projects. Where evaluation is associated with genuine learning, especially to ensure that mistakes are not repeated, it adds great value.

The careful measurement of the impact of reforms, whether funded by aid or domestic resources has been at the heart of *impact evaluation* which seeks to provide the metrics for the more effective use of interventions. Impact evaluation aims to attribute changes to particular interventions by comparing what happens with cases where the intervention did not occur. Its increasing popularity reflects the desire of donors—particularly the new private philanthropists who come from a business background—to measure outcomes.

The introduction of *randomized control trials* (RCTs) has added a powerful new method to the toolbox employed by development experts. The proponents of these trials aim to conduct what are considered to be field experiments that replicate, as far as possible, research methods originally employed in medicine to evaluate the effectiveness of new drugs. Proponents of RCTs argue that focusing on pragmatic projects can provide tested solutions and end the uncertainties associated with large complex projects. Among the first applications of these tools were in the design of conditional cash transfer programmes to improve education and health outcomes. The Bolsa Familia programme in Brazil and Prospera programme in Mexico (formerly known as Oportunidades and Progresa respectively) demonstrated the potential for randomized trials and these methods have subsequently been utilized in many countries. Abhijit Banerjee and Esther Duflo in their book *Poor Economics* argue that it is possible to break cycles of persistent poverty and establish new growth trajectories by providing poor people and policymakers with effective, valid information.

RCTs have much to offer. However, as Martin Ravallion and others have argued the complexities of development mean that not everything is susceptible to randomized experiments. Reliance on these tools can shift development policy towards interventions that can be measured. This may lead to an excessive focus on short-term interventions in those countries or projects where time series and comparative data exists and governance is relative stable. This reliance discriminates against regions or places where there is weak governance and poor or non-existent data. As a result of data shortcomings, the poorest countries and places may be left behind inadvertently. It is also not possible to construct randomized trials for national reform efforts, such as judicial or macroeconomic reforms, which cannot be done only in certain localities and for which there is seldom a counterfactual. Where an intervention improves lives, such as the distribution of malaria bed nets, vaccinations, or HIV/AIDS antiretroviral drugs, the deliberate decision not to distribute the lifesaving drugs or therapies to all potential recipients in order to conduct randomized trials raises profound ethical questions for policymakers. No tool can address all needs and understanding the limitations of randomized trials is vital in order to appreciate their powerful potential contribution to development.

6

❦

Sustainable Development

The environment and development are intimately related yet this relationship has only recently come to the centre of development concerns. In 1972, the United Nations Conference on the Human Environment signalled an early recognition of the importance of the environment. In 1987, the World Commission for the Environment and Development published its findings in *Our Common Future* which became known as the Brundtland Report, after its Chair Harlem Brundtland. The Commission introduced the concept of *sustainable development* to a wide audience. This recognizes that while economic growth has contributed to improved living standards and life expectancy for many people around the world, it has adversely affected the environment by depleting (or irreversibly damaging) the natural resource base and that in the longer term this undermines future growth prospects and living standards.

In the three decades since the Brundtland Report was published, both growth and environmental destruction have accelerated. At least half of the world's forests have been lost, and while the rate of deforestation has slowed, it is still alarmingly high; net deforestation was 5.2 million hectares per year between 2000 and 2010, down from 8.3 million hectares per year between 1990 and 2000. Every year around 12 million hectares of land is lost due to land degradation and desertification, costing around $42 billion in lost incomes. Water scarcity affects between 1 and 2 billion people worldwide; and around 660 million people continue to lack access to improved drinking water. Overfishing has seriously depleted fish stocks, with around 85 per cent of global fish stocks overexploited, depleted, fully exploited, or in recovery from exploitation. Twenty per cent of the world's coral reefs have been lost and an additional 20 per cent degraded. The loss of bio-diversity as a result of human activity is widely recognized as posing a significant threat to development. The Millennium Ecosystem Assessment in 2005 highlighted the threat of extinction of 10 to 30 per cent of all mammal, bird, and amphibian species due to past human activity. Subsequent analysis by the International Union for Conservation of Nature (IUCN) has identified even more dramatic biodiversity losses and threats to development.

The significance of sulphur, lead, mercury, nitrates, and many other pollutants have only recently started to be recognized. The lags between the activities and their impact becoming known can be very long indeed, as shown by our belated understanding of the threat posed by greenhouse gases to the ozone layer and climate. It has taken two centuries to understand the consequences of growth based on fossil fuels and the consequent cumulative effects of carbon emissions on climate systems. The implications for development are just beginning to be understood.

The extent to which *climate change* will impact on development depends crucially on the limits that can be established for global emissions of carbon dioxide and greenhouse gases. Keeping to within a 2-degree-Celsius temperature increase over the pre-industrial average is a minimum required to prevent dangerous climate change. This requires radical changes in energy systems and the achievement of zero carbon emissions within a few decades, yet some scientists note this ambitious ceiling may still result in destabilizing climate change globally and may well result in catastrophic climate change for many communities.

Climate change is already affecting the world's poorest and most vulnerable people. Poor countries and poor people tend to be concentrated on the most fragile and vulnerable lands. They also lack the capacity and resources to cope. The *mitigation* of the impact of climate change through limiting greenhouse gases is essential. But as climate change is already happening, and even if it can be limited to 2 degrees Celsius, it will have a potentially catastrophic impact on the development prospects of many people. Interventions to improve *adaptation* to climate change are therefore becoming a development focus at both the national and international level. This includes interventions in flood and coastal defences, irrigation and water storage, stress-resistant crops, retrofitting of homes, offices and other buildings to reduce heat absorption, and other measures to try to offset the impact of climate change.

Ocean rise is likely to have a dramatic impact on low-lying islands, with the possibility of the Maldives and a number of other countries completely disappearing. Coastal plains are likely to be similarly inundated. With over 25 per cent of Bangladesh less than one metre above sea level and the majority of the population living in the fertile delta area, an increase in ocean levels poses a fundamental threat to Bangladesh as it does to an estimated one billion coastal people, mainly in Asia.

Climate change is likely to pose a major threat to agricultural systems, as it increases the instability of weather patterns, leading to significant fluctuations in maximum and minimum temperatures, winds, rainfall distribution and intensity, and other critical determinants of agricultural productivity. Even small variations in seasonal and daily patterns at critical periods of the growing season can have a devastating impact on crops.

Water scarcity is similarly likely to be exacerbated by climate change, requiring major improvements in the efficiency of water use, not least as over half of water that is piped is estimated to be lost due to leakage. Investments in recycling and in more efficient irrigation systems are also required.

The development of energy systems which radically reduce carbon emissions requires not only rapid growth in renewable sources—wind, solar, hydro, tidal, biomass, and other—but also the retrofitting of existing systems to reduce carbon emissions. Increasing the efficiency of energy use and reducing the carbon intensity of growth is vital too, requiring urgent action including the retrofitting of buildings and transformation of transport systems.

Limits to Growth?

The Brundtland report challenged the view that more is always better. It built on the work of the Club of Rome, and its influential 1972 book on *Limits to Growth* which posed a powerful challenge to conventional ideas on economic growth and development by showing that development had resulted in water and air pollution, deforestation, desertification, and biodiversity loss. It identified that there was a diminishing capacity of the natural environment to act as a waste-absorbing 'sink'. Subsequently, industrial output, population, and energy use have all increased dramatically, resulting in a rapid increase in carbon, methane, and sulphur dioxide emissions. With increasing evidence of climate change and biodiversity loss, as well as the many other spill-over effects of rapid development, the challenge of sustainability is beginning to belatedly enter the mainstream of development thinking. In only a handful of countries, and most notably in China, have these concerns become central to development debates.

Echoing the work of the Club of Rome, Johan Rockström and others at the Stockholm Resilience Centre have sought to define *planetary boundaries*. This work together with that of Global Footprint and other organizations highlights the fact that in many areas we are already exceeding the Earth's carrying capacity and that further development along current trajectories is unsustainable.

There is some evidence of an 'Environmental Kuznets Curve' by which pollution intensity first increases and then decreases over the development cycle. Industrial growth first damages the environment, but as incomes rise and priorities change, countries increasingly address environmental problems. Many economists continue to believe in the ability of markets to address these problems by investing in both human and natural capital that generates new technologies. The Environmental Kuznets Curve implies growth is good for the environment in the long run. It draws on Kuznets' hypothesis that economic growth would at first exacerbate inequality, but later, at higher per capita incomes, inequality would decrease. The environmental variant of this suggests a similar relationship between growth and environmental degradation: economic growth might negatively impact the environment as countries become wealthier and incomes rise, but this environmental degradation will decline once incomes rise and citizens and regulators constrain polluting industries. While there is some evidence to support this contention for certain environmental impacts, such as water and air pollution, the pattern does not apply to all pollutants. The richest countries account for many of the most severe environmental problems, and per capita greenhouse gas emissions for the high-income countries are much higher than for middle- or lower-income countries.

The unique development challenge of the coming decades is that even if the current development trajectories eventually lead to lower negative spillovers, there is now a very real risk that we would have destroyed global ecosystems long before getting there. There are a number of reasons for this. First, in many critical regions pollution is so far above sustainable levels that its decline is insufficient to offset the risks. This is the case with carbon emissions in the United States, which have finally slowed, but at levels which are too high. Second, there could be a severely negative global impact as very large numbers of people enter the peak pollution phase of development. China and India together have around two and a half billion people, and even relatively low levels of per capita pollution cumulatively have a catastrophic cumulative global impact.

Reconciling the demands of growth with those of ecological and other natural systems requires that the spillover impact of market choices is reflected in pricing and resource allocation. Among the approaches to achieve this end are the *polluter pays principle*; whereby those responsible for degrading the environment should bear the full costs. The valuation of environmental services provides a means by which those who conserve environmental resources should receive compensation from those who benefit. (An example of this is Costa Rica's Pago por Servicios Ambientales.) It has been estimated that the annual monetary value of ecosystem services is a staggering $33 trillion, equivalent to nearly half of global income. Only a tiny fraction of this is reflected in payment for the services or the protection of the systems which yield these unrecognized and unrewarded services for humanity.

The widening scholarly and policy debates on the definition and measurement of development in recent decades has been enriched by a growing concern regarding the relationship between current choices and future outcomes, for people and also for ecological and natural resource systems. The rate at which governments and firms discount future expected benefits can make a major difference to how the future is valued. Along with a growing recognition that economics alone cannot provide adequate insights into development has come the recognition that the economic toolbox is unable to grapple adequately with a wide range of vital questions regarding future prospects.

Economic models typically value the preferences of future generations at a discounted rate to the current generation. The value that should be attached to the future is a subject of considerable debate, as evidenced by Nordhaus's criticism of the low discount used by Stern in his analysis of climate change. Having a lower discount rate and placing a higher value on the future means we pay more attention to longer-term goals and to preserving natural systems. Uncertainty about how actions today may impact on future generations should also provide a powerful reason to sustain natural resources. Applied to climate change, this implies that, even if the risk is low that current policies will ruin the prospects for future generations, we should adopt the *precautionary principle* to reduce these potentially disastrous risks.

Governments and international organizations have taken some actions to protect and restore the environment. The 1992 United Nations Conference on the Environment and Development (Rio Agenda 21) placed people at the centre of sustainable development and emphasized the relationship between poverty and environmental degradation. International organizations such as the United

Nations Environment Programme (UNEP) and the Global Environmental Facility provide much-needed advice and finance for addressing environmental concerns in development. There is a vital role to play for NGOs, such as IUCN, Greenpeace, the World Wide Fund for Nature and The Nature Conservancy—which is now the biggest non-government landowner in the United States—as well as research groups, including those in the CGIAR agricultural research system and the many groups working in universities and national research centres around the world. These groups have their strengths and weaknesses, and there is room for efficiency improvements as well as greater coordination, not least to address the orphan issues which are not adequately covered by any agency. However, given the scale and urgency of the need for new ideas, technologies, and finance to address the needs of sustainable development, much greater investment in environmental awareness and protection is required.

Numerous international treaties have been signed and conferences convened to address environmental issues, with a number of these focused on the nexus of development and the environment. The United Nations Framework Convention on Climate Change treaty was adopted at the 1992 Earth Summit. In total 196 signatories have agreed to limit greenhouse gas emissions, but despite the annual Conference of the Parties (COP) meetings, inadequate progress has been made. A small minority of signatories have achieved their targets. Some countries such as the United States and Australia (neither of which ratified the treaty) argued that the targets would seriously damage their economies and that other countries (India, China) must make firm commitments. The Paris COP21 meetings in December 2015 for the first time saw 196 countries agreeing to set a goal of limiting global warming to 2 degrees Celsius compared to pre-industrial levels. This will require not only acting on the promises made in Paris, but going well beyond them to ensure a truly decarbonized global economy with zero net anthropogenic greenhouse gas emissions within the next thirty to fifty years. Achieving this implies that the majority of existing fossil fuel reserves are unlikely to ever be exploited. It also implies that new power stations or other investments which rely on fossil fuel energy sources are likely to have a curtailed lifespan. For the many developing countries that are still climbing the steepest part of the energy curve, decarbonizing while meeting the energy demands of development presents an extraordinarily difficult—and yet vital—national and global development challenge.

7

⟨⟨⟨⟩⟩⟩

Globalization and Development

Globalization is interpreted in many ways and may be understood as an increase in the impact of human activities that span national borders. Globalization is a process associated with the integration of societies and may be measured in terms of flows across national borders. These flows may be economic, cultural, political, social, technological, environmental, human (travel and migration), biological (diseases), or virtual (cyber, telecommunications, and internet). The principal economic flows are finance, trade, aid, migration, and intellectual property and ideas.

The relationship between globalization and development is contested. For some, globalization is a powerful force for poverty reduction and has led to leaps in life expectancy and other key dimensions of development. For others, globalization has negative implications and is seen as a source of growing inequality, poverty, unemployment, and environmental destruction. Advocates of both perspectives can point to evidence to support their views as in practice the flows that represent globalization can have both positive and negative impacts. The outcome depends on the policies and preparedness of societies to manage the flows to ensure that the positive potential is harvested while the negative consequences are managed and mitigated.

Finance and Development

Global financial flows are an important resource for developing countries. These capital flows augment domestic savings and can contribute to investment, growth, financial sector development, technological transfer, and poverty reduction. Aside from aid, there are four different types of capital flows. The first is *foreign direct investment*, the second *equity investment*, the third *bond finance and debt issuance* and the fourth commercial *bank lending*. In practice, these may be combined and mixed in various hybrid formulations. In 2015, the total of these private flows to developing countries is estimated to be around one trillion dollars (Figure 8).

Foreign direct investment involves the acquisition of over 10 per cent of a foreign-based enterprise, which usually implies managerial participation in the foreign business. *Equity* investment involves the purchase of shares in foreign enterprises. Where the shareholding is too small to involve managerial participation, it is termed equity portfolio investment. These investments are indirect rather than direct investments and are undertaken to gain exposure to the foreign firm rather than to exercise managerial control.

Private equity is a form of investment in which investors buy shares in unlisted companies which are not publicly traded on a stock exchange. If they are listed, the private equity investment leads to a buyout of a publicly listed company and its delisting. Private equity investments are typically made by a private equity firm or very wealthy individual, whereas portfolio investments may be made by large numbers of investors through purchases of listed shares or by mutual funds and financial brokers.

Bond finance is a form of debt issuance that involves governments or firms issuing bonds, which are purchased by investors who loan the issuer money for a defined period of time at a variable or fixed interest rate. Bonds are used by governments, companies, cities, states, and other institutions to raise money and can be issued in either domestic currency or foreign currency. The risks associated with bonds not being repaid are known as default risks, and are evaluated by *credit rating agencies*. International investment in bond markets in developing countries requires the establishment of *credit ratings* for the countries and companies. The number of ratings in these markets has grown rapidly in recent decades from barely a dozen countries, to include over one hundred countries. The establishment of emerging market benchmarks, such as the JP Morgan Emerging Market Bond Index, has increased the exposure of developing countries to mutual fund, pension, and other pooled investment managers, increasing the liquidity and fundraising potential of issuers in these markets. International investors typically require *investment grade* ratings from two agencies. Investment grade is classified as BBB- or higher by

Standard & Poor's and by Fitch, and Baa3 or higher by Moodys.

Commercial bank lending is another form of debt, but whereas bonds can be bought and sold, and are therefore tradable assets, bank lending is not tradable. Until the 1990s, commercial bank lending was the principal source of finance for many middle-income countries and for firms. Subsequently, equity portfolio investment and bond finance flows have become more significant. The volatility of these flows was demonstrated following the Asian financial crisis in 1997 and again during the global financial crisis of 2007–9 and again more recently. From July 2009 until the end of June 2014, a net total of $2.2 trillion in capital flowed into the fifteen largest emerging markets. In subsequent months, changing sentiment and the impact of the tightening of monetary policy in the United States led to a reversal of the flows, with net capital outflows from emerging economies expected to amount to $540 billion in 2015.

Since 2000, the United States Treasury has been by far the biggest issuer of bonds, and owes over $13 trillion, of which over $6 trillion is to foreigners. China holds reserves of over $3 trillion in United States Treasuries. As a result of transactions such as this by the United States, European, and other advanced countries, developing countries have become net exporters of capital. This turns on its head earlier views that the advanced countries would save more as they became more developed, and that capital should flow to developing countries where investment needs are highest and the levels of savings lower than in advanced economies.

In recent years, the returns on fixed-income, debt, and bond products have declined in advanced countries. Meanwhile developing countries have become more attractive investment destinations as a result of their improved economic performance and robust growth, relative to the advanced economies. In the first five months of 2015, developing country governments raised a record $210 billion in sovereign bonds, double the level of issuance of the comparable period in 2010. Private companies increasingly have turned to bond markets rather than bank lending to raise finance with firms in developing countries having raised over $2.4 trillion through corporate bonds. Private equity has similarly grown rapidly as a source of finance for many developing countries. Whereas developing countries accounted for barely 10 per cent of private equity flows in the period to 2010, since then they have accounted for over twenty per cent of total private equity fundraising. Global private equity fundraising in 2014 amounted to almost $500 billion, of which over $50 billion was destined for emerging markets, out of which around $3.2 billion went to sub-Saharan Africa.

Numerous private equity funds have been created which attract investment from a combination of institutional and private investors and mobilize these savings for investment in businesses in developing countries. The funds typically have an investable period of around ten years, following which the fund managers exit and sell the mature business to others or float it on stock markets. Funds tend to designate particular sectors (mining, agriculture, health, or other) and size (medium or large investments) and countries. While funds investing in China have dominated the market in recent years, other regions have been able to attract sizeable portfolios. Private equity flows to Africa increased from an average of around half a billion dollars per annum prior to 2005, to well over one billion dollars per year in the subsequent decade, and in the period 2013 to 2015 exceeded three billion per year. Over the past two decades, private equity has grown rapidly, providing a new source of finance for private investments in developing countries, with cumulative investments exceeding $30 billion in Africa alone.

Trade and Development

Trade is a key dimension of globalization. The promotion of equitable trade includes improving access to key international markets for developing countries. The opening up of markets through the removal of trade barriers such as tariffs and subsidies has the potential to contribute far more towards development than international aid flows.

Agricultural protectionism takes many forms and its pernicious impact was touched upon in Chapter 4. Subsidies of around $250 billion per year are given to grain and farmers of other protected agricultural commodities in Europe, the United States, and Japan. As a result of these subsidies, each day the average Swiss cow benefits from subsidies which are much greater than the daily income of over 300 million Africans. In addition, quotas on the import of certain products, such as North African tomatoes and citrus, as well as tariff and non-tariff barriers, undermine the ability of developing countries to compete in agricultural products in the protected markets. As a result of these measures, the products produced by poor people on average face double the tariffs that producers in rich countries face.

Tariff escalation is the process by which the tariffs imposed by importers increase with the level of processing. This undermines the potential of developing countries to increase the value associated with their production by processing their raw material exports. For example, whereas West African exporters face a low import tariff for raw coffee or cocoa, they face at least 20 per cent higher tariffs when they export manufactured goods, such as instant coffee powder or chocolate. This significantly diminishes their incomes and opportunities.

A number of advanced countries, including New Zealand, Australia, and Canada, have low levels of domestic protection and lower barriers to imports. However, the largest advanced markets, notably the European Union, United States, and Japan have trade policies that undermine the prospects of many exporters by frustrating exports to their markets. These policies, by reducing the prospects for adding value through processing, simultaneously increase instability in world food and agricultural markets by encouraging developing countries to specialize in non-protected commodities, such as rubber, cocoa, and oil-palms.

Agricultural protectionism not only impacts negatively on poor people in poor countries but also has a negative impact on people in the richer countries. In the United States and Europe for example, the cost of sugar, dairy products, and cooking oil is well above global market levels, so that the average European pays over 1,000 euros more per year for their food than they need to ($1,000 in the United States). As poor people pay a higher share of their income on these foodstuffs than rich people, these subsidies have a regressive social impact, and increase inequality in rich countries, as well as between rich and poor countries and within poor countries.

Achieving a more even playing field is a central objective of the Doha Round of Trade Negotiations that was initiated in 2001. The apparently insurmountable obstacles to the completion of the Trade Round have meant that trade barriers continue to undermine the development agenda. Protectionism also serves as a drag on global growth. Estimates suggest that the gains in global income from the Doha trade negotiations could be over $160 billion, just over a quarter of which will accrue to developing countries.

While in the advanced economies agricultural protectionism is often justified as helping small farmers—thereby improving food security for poor people and protecting the countryside—in reality the opposite is the case. In Europe and the United States over 80 per cent of the benefits of agricultural protection go to under 5 per cent of farmers, with small numbers of well-placed farmers earning millions of euros or dollars a year from taxpayers and consumers. As these subsidies contribute to higher land values, agricultural protectionism serves to increase the intensity of land use, and encourage excessive application of fertilizers and pesticides. Protectionism in the United States and Europe has led to a concentration of land ownership, as it mainly funds large farmers. The small farmers who produce crops that are not subsidized find they are increasingly uncompetitive. While many voters imagine that the policies support an image of the idyllic countryside, the opposite tends to be the case, as the policies contribute to excessive nitrogen and other chemical applications, and the pollution of rivers and ground water. Meanwhile monocropping leads to a loss of biodiversity in regions enjoying the most protection. From both a domestic and international development perspective, the policies are economically, environmentally, and ethically nonsensical. They survive because a tiny minority—well under 1 per cent of the voting population—is able to exercise lobbying and other powers to maintain vested interests.

Many developing countries are under-represented at the WTO or lack the capacity to take full advantage of the negotiation process. More needs to be done to address power imbalances within the governance structure of the WTO and to improve the negotiating capacity of poor countries. The required investments in capacity include legal training. This is provided by initiatives such as the Advisory Centre on WTO Law and the International Trade Centre's World Trade Net.

Trade in knowledge and ideas is another important area for reform, with Trade Related Intellectual Property Rights (TRIPS) becoming more important to developing countries. It is often argued that intellectual property rights drive innovation and contribute to growth by creating incentives to pursue new ideas. The problem for developing countries is that intellectual property rights are a legally sanctioned restraint of trade. They can lead to the monopolization of ideas and innovation by first comers. Developing countries fear that countries with better endowed research and legal systems will prevent affordable access to technologies which are crucial for development. Two areas of intellectual property protection that require urgent attention are pharmaceuticals and agricultural research.

More needs to be done to improve the availability, price, and effectiveness of essential drugs for tackling HIV/AIDS and tropical diseases such as malaria, cholera, and bilharzia. In 2001, Brazil, India, and South Africa attracted global media attention when they challenged United States patents which raised the price of antiretroviral (ARV) drugs to AIDS patients in their countries. Since then flexibilities have been built into TRIPS and the price of frontline ARVs has come down.

The lack of purchasing power in developing countries (especially Africa) severely limits commercial incentives to conduct research and invest in drugs intended to prevent diseases that are prevalent in low-income countries. Average per capita health expenditure in sub-Saharan Africa is currently below $100 per year, whereas average per capita health expenditure in the United States is $9,145—over ninety times higher. Even where drugs are available, affordability is often a problem. So, for example, the Measles and Rubella Initiative (founded in 2001) makes use of one of the most cost-effective vaccines available, which can be purchased and administered for just $1.50. Although the initiative has reduced the number of children dying from measles worldwide from 562,000 in 2000 by a factor of four, the disease still killed an estimated 145,700 children in 2013 due to lack of money and resources.

Agricultural research and technology is vital for developing countries. Access to seeds and appropriate agricultural technology mirrors the problems in health. The global biotech market is currently worth $5.5 billion per year and reaps 60 per cent of its profit from bio-seeds; patents have become concentrated in a small number of companies. It is estimated that over 70 per cent of all agricultural biotechnology patents are owned by the top five companies in the field and that one company accounts for 90 per cent of genetically modified seeds in the world today.

Technology and Development

The relationship between development and technological progress is complex. Technological progress embodies new ideas and is bundled with an often wide range of skill, process, infrastructure, cultural, and other changes. Separating the specific role of technology as a driver of development at times may therefore exaggerate its role. The wheel, gunpowder, printing, the steam engine, the telegraph, penicillin, and the Internet have all had a profound impact on development. Yet, their implications are highly uneven. No technology is a panacea and the adoption, adaptation, and dissemination of technological changes need to be seen within wider institutional, economic, and social settings.

Technology has come to be associated with 'hardware'—such as computers, machines, and equipment—but it is also 'software', including the systems, methods, and processes which are used to achieve particular scientific and other goals, or are associated with the production of goods and services.

The adoption of new technologies is a key dimension of development. So too is the adaptation and modification of technologies to meet local needs and be applicable for use within particular societies. Skills, attitudes, and infrastructure have a strong influence on this diffusion between and within countries. As does the regulatory and policy environment, both at the international and national level. Trade in goods and services and flows of capital are often packaged with ideas and innovation and there is an extensive literature on the role of technology transfer in foreign investment.

As we have seen, the idea of *intellectual property rights* is amongst the most controversial in development. Figure 11 shows that the global share of patents is highly unequal and mirrors the trend previously observed in agricultural and biotechnology markets. This means that the problem for latecomers is that patents can restrict the flow of ideas and the application of vital technologies in areas such as health, food security, education, trade, industrial policy, traditional knowledge, biotechnology, information technology, and the entertainment and media industries. The other side of the argument is that protecting firms' intellectual property can spur innovation in these industries. Striking a balance, particularly in a world of powerful players and vested interests, is a crucial development challenge.

The extension of intellectual property protection to traditional knowledge, folklore, and culture would allow developing countries to benefit from their own indigenous

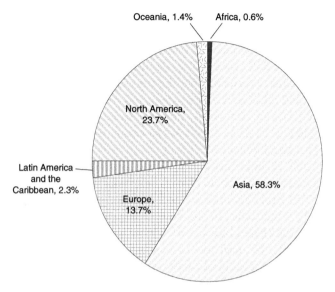

Figure 11 Share of patents across regions (2013).

knowledge and enhance the commercial value of poor people's knowledge. The use of plants and remedies from developing countries in modern medicines, or of craft designs from traditional communities in Africa or Latin America is seldom, if ever, rewarded with the payment of a royalty, as would apply to designers and artists in richer countries.

The use of information and communications technology for development, labelled by the experts as 'ICT4D', can significantly improve opportunities and allow societies to leapfrog the absence of fixed-line infrastructure to ensure high rates of penetration in both urban and rural communities. In Kenya M-PESA has provided financial services to previously neglected poor communities, as well as to the urban middle class using mobile phones, dramatically increasing access while cutting the costs of financial transfers and other services. Elsewhere, ICT is being used to communicate market prices, improve health, and to offer a widening range of e-services. To ensure that ICT serves to assist development it is necessary to overcome the 'digital divide'. A key element of this is the provision of high-speed broadband coverage to often remote poor communities.

The term 'intermediate technology' was articulated by E. F. Schumacher in his book *Small is Beautiful* and has been transferred into a development context by those that argue for the need for 'appropriate technology' which is designed to meet local needs, and avoid capital and energy intensive imports which cannot be operated with local skills or energy sources, which should preferably be renewable.

The world has witnessed the rapid pace of scientific invention, with advances in computing, nano medicine, stem cell research, genetics, artificial intelligence, robotics, and computing all pointing to the potential for science to address critical challenges. Optimists point to the potential of these and many other technologies to meet the needs of development. Others worry about the potential for the accelerating pace of change to leave many poor countries and poor people further and further behind. Even in the rich countries, they may well widen inequality, with those that fail to effectively adopt or adapt to technological change finding they are replaced by machine intelligence and robots which perform a widening range of tasks. There is a real risk that technological change may exacerbate inequality as large groups of individuals may be disconnected due to illiteracy or absence of broadband, find that they are unemployed and that their skills are no longer relevant, or become otherwise excluded from the benefits of change.

Technological change provides immense possibilities, but technologies need to be embedded in societies. The availability and applicability of appropriate technologies, together with the quality and adaptability of complementary education, skills, regulations, and institutions will determine the extent to which technology contributes to meeting development challenges or creates new obstacles to development.

International Regulation and Cooperation

The prevention of transfer pricing and of tax avoidance is important in building a sound revenue base for development. Transfer pricing—or mispricing—involves manipulating the prices charged for goods and services sold between subsidiaries controlled by the same company. By charging high prices, multinationals can move profits out of one country and into another in order to take advantage of low or zero tax havens. Large corporations have also taken advantage of a complex range of other tax avoidance initiatives including loopholes, tax shelters, and financial arrangements (such as artificially high interest rate payments to controlled entities) in order to minimize their tax bills.

While corporations and financial flows are increasingly globalized, governments are constrained to operate within national jurisdictions. International rules and regulations are at times developed to operate across national borders, but these international agreements tend to evolve much more slowly than the flows of cross-border activities. This is because it takes considerable time to achieve cooperation and negotiate treaties, not least when countries perceive a very different interest in the outcomes.

Governments compete to provide particularly attractive tax shelters and other incentives for footloose corporations to locate in their jurisdictions. Whereas the cooperation of a small number of large countries can make a big difference in certain areas, such as climate change or Security Council reform, in other areas the cooperation of many small countries is essential. So, for example, to ensure that companies pay their fair share of tax, tiny islands and enclaves, such as the Cayman Islands, Monaco, Luxembourg, and Lichtenstein, would have to stop serving as tax havens for global firms and wealthy individuals.

In 2012, several major global companies were publicly criticized for not paying their fair share of tax. Amongst those singled out by the media were Apple, which was alleged to have paid only 2 per cent corporation tax on profits outside the United States, Google, which allegedly avoided a tax bill of $2 billion in 2011, by moving nearly $10 billion into a unit in Bermuda, a jurisdiction that levies no corporate income tax, Amazon which allegedly paid no corporation tax in the United Kingdom on income of £3.3 billion; and Starbucks which was reported to have paid £8.6

million in corporation taxes in fourteen years on United Kingdom earnings of £3 billion (a rate of under 1 per cent).

Tax avoidance is especially costly for low-income countries, which are in urgent need of financial revenues but lack the resources for effective tax enforcement. The estimated resulting tax avoidance could amount to a quarter of total corporate profit-tax receipts in rich countries, and more in poor ones. Following the media storm in 2012, the G8 and G20 pledged to make a real difference in addressing tax avoidance by sharing information and pooling resources. The proposals eventually endorsed by the G20 finance ministers eighteen months later (in Cairns, Australia, September 2014) did not amount to the much discussed unitary tax, which would have obliged companies to pay tax in the countries where profits and sales were actually generated. The more limited proposals nevertheless have the backing of forty-four countries—accounting for 90 per cent of the world's economy. They include the sharing of basic information about multinationals (such as assets, sales, profits, and employees) in the hope of spotting tax avoidance as well as measures to clamp down on transfer pricing, treaty shopping (arrangements that allow firms to derive benefits from a tax treaty, despite not being resident in either country that is party to it) and hybrid mismatches, whereby companies claim double deductions by classifying financial instruments as debts in some countries and equity in others.

Actions which follow from this information may require legal reform or treaty changes. However, even when such treaties are signed, they are not necessarily implemented by national governments. Indeed, countries find it much easier to sign agreements than to implement them nationally, leading to a widening disconnect between what appears in international law and treaties and the implementation by the signatory countries.

It has been argued that the more globalization encourages flows of finance and trade, the more illicit commerce—estimated by Moisés Naím as around 10 per cent of all flows—also flourishes. Among the flows which undermine development are those in small arms, toxic waste, slave and sex trafficking, ivory, and other illicit trade. Not all trade is beneficial and control over harmful illicit trade is a necessary dimension of cooperation to ensure that globalization helps—and not hinders—the achievement of development objectives.

Among the top arms importers in per capita terms are many of the world's poorest nations. As we have seen, the resulting violence has culminated in numerous conflicts and countless fatalities (Chapter 4). The regulation of the arms trade—not least to conflict zones—requires more attention. Trade in hazardous waste and endangered species, which can have serious environmental implications, is another area for action as is the slave trade, sex trafficking, and other illicit forms of trade. A startling fact is that it has been estimated that there are more slaves alive today than at the end of the Atlantic Slave Trade more than two centuries ago. According to the Walk Free Foundation, an estimated 35 million people around the world are trapped in modern forms of slavery, including 14 million in India, 5.6 million in sub-Saharan Africa, and 3.2 million in China.

International Migration and Development

Migration historically has been the most powerful means to escape poverty. It has led to the survival of our species when threatened by natural disasters and is a primary reason for the development of the civilizations that have given rise to our societies. The invention of passports in the early twentieth century, and the subsequent creation of over a hundred countries, with increasingly impenetrable borders, has meant that the relationship between migration and development is changing. Although the share of the world's population migrating has remained relatively stable at around 3 per cent, this is due in large part to an increase in the number of countries. The ability of individuals to use migration to escape poverty has declined over time as border controls have increased. International migration and development nevertheless remain intertwined.

There are currently around 250 million international migrants. Of these about 91 million have moved between developing countries, and a further 86 million from developing to advanced economies, with the balance of 73 million being between advanced economies and from advanced to developing countries. The main motive for migration is economic, although millions of people also move across borders to study, reunite with their family, and to escape repression, discrimination, natural disasters, and other risks. In many cases these push-and-pull factors are inter-related. Whatever the causes of international migration, the consequences for development in both the sending and receiving countries are profound.

Remittances are a tangible reflection of migration. These are financial transfers that migrants send to their families and dependents back home. Because migrants tend to send more when the recipients need this support most and times are tough, remittances exercise a counter-cyclical role. A share of remittances is invested in education, housing, and other long-term investments which support development.

In 1990, recorded remittance transfers to developing countries were about $31 billion and in 2015 they are estimated to have reached $436 billion. The apparent fourteen-fold increase in part is attributable to better measurement. Whereas remittances previously may not have been recorded or were channelled through informal flows, increased surveillance of financial flows, together with the rise of specialist remittance agents, has led to the increased declaration of remittances. In 2014, the largest flows were to India (over $70 billion) and China ($64 billion). For smaller countries, the impacts are proportionally more significant, with remittances accounting for well over 20 per cent of GDP in a number of developing countries, including Tajikistan (49 per cent), Kyrgyz Republic (32 per cent), Nepal (25 per cent), Moldova (25 per cent), Tonga (24 per cent), Haiti (21 per cent), Armenia (21 per cent), Lesotho (20 per cent), Samoa (20 per cent), and the Gambia (20 per cent). Remittances are private flows in which individuals voluntarily send funds to their personal choice of beneficiaries. They should not be classed as aid or directed into official coffers. Reducing the cost of making remittance transfers, which typically absorbs over 10 per cent of the value, has highly positive development impacts, as it increases the value of funds received by the beneficiaries and typically is spent on improving their welfare.

The *brain drain* of skilled graduates and professionals leaving developing countries can undermine development prospects, but the impact of these flows is not necessarily negative and can be consistent with development. The Philippines, for example, is the largest exporter of nurses, but has one of the highest ratios of nurses to its population, due to the investment in the training of nurses, and the return of nurses from working abroad. While the brain drain may have negative consequences, the ability of graduates and professionals to work in other countries can also lead to higher levels of provision of professional education (stimulated by the desire to migrate), return migration (which brings new technologies and skills), and strong networks with diasporas (that encourage investment and economic aid), amongst other benefits. Diasporas may also provide a powerful source of political support as is evident in the role of the Taiwanese and Israeli diasporas.

If international migration is managed appropriately, it can exercise a powerful positive influence on development and be beneficial for both the sending and receiving countries.

Country-level studies in recipient countries suggest that migrants are more productive and flexible than the indigenous population and that they stimulate growth, spur innovation, add to cultural diversity, and contrary to popular belief, are net contributors to the public purse. At the global level studies suggest that even a small increase in migration would produce significant gains for the global economy. The World Bank, in 2005, estimated that a modest rise in migration equal

149

to 3 per cent of the global workforce between 2005 and 2025 would generate global gains of $365 billion, with two-thirds of the gains accruing to developing countries. Completely opening borders, some economists suggest, would produce gains as high as $39 trillion over twenty-five years.

International migration requires more attention than it has received from the international community and far greater cooperation between nation states is required to enhance the benefits of international labour mobility, to realize the potential for development driven by remittances, and to manage the downside of the brain drain for developing countries. Initiatives such as the Global Forum on Migration and Development and the International Organization for Migration have made significant contributions, but there is no United Nations organization responsible for development and migration, which remains an orphan of the global system. Even relatively simple questions, such as the definition of migrants, or the transfer of pension rights across borders are not subjects of global agreements. Meanwhile, the international rights of migrants are neglected.

The intersection of migration and development raises profound questions as to the commitment of those that have enjoyed the fruits of migration and development to share them more widely. The failure of most European countries to give access to desperate migrants fleeing wars and destitution in Syria, Eritrea, and other countries raises profound questions regarding commitments to development. Everyone on our fragile planet shared a common migratory ancestry, not least with the East Africans who were our forbears. The anti-migrant sentiment in many countries—

rich and poor—against foreigners may be understandable but it is misplaced. Allowing migrants to die in the Mediterranean or South Asian seas reflects the unevenness in global development, and a denial of our common human origins. Our ability to migrate is what makes us human and accounts for our peopling of the world and our civilizations. Until the options became severely limited with the increased number of countries, borders, and restrictions, migration was the most powerful impetus for individual and national development.

Refugees and Development

Civil war, genocide, and other forms of persecution have led to a rise in the number of refugees since the late 1970s. A *refugee* is someone who seeks protection outside his or her country of nationality due to fear of persecution for social, political, religious, or ethnic reasons; refugees are protected under the United Nations *Convention on the Status of Refugees* (1951). The number of refugees has grown rapidly in recent years, from approximately 15 million in 2012 to over 20 million in 2015. Developing countries host over 86 per cent of refugees. The largest single group of refugees, the 5.1 million registered Palestinians, date from those who lost both home and their means of livelihood as a result of the 1948 conflict and creation of the state of Israel and associated eviction of Palestinians.

The number of *forcibly displaced people* was estimated at 60 million in 2014, with the difference between this number and the number of refugees reflecting the fact that most people seek sanctuary by moving to another location within their own country, rather than to another country. The number of people forced to leave their homes is greater than at any time since the Second World War. In 2015, the arrival of well over a million desperate refugees from Syria, Afghanistan, Eritrea, and elsewhere posed a major challenge to European governments. Germany alone received over one million refugees in 2015, and over twice the total of all fifty other European countries. Turkey, Lebanon, and Jordan, meanwhile, are home to over 3 million refugees, and globally over 80 per cent of refugees are hosted by developing countries, which greatly adds to their development challenge. In the face of the refugees' desperate situation and hazardous journeys, which have resulted in the deaths of many thousands, European countries and commentators have been divided in their response, at times ignoring the legal imperatives and ethical obligations to protect refugees.

The legal definition of a refugee is fairly narrow; the United Nations Refugee Agency (UNHRC) has identified several other categories of 'people of concern' including 'internally displaced persons', and 'stateless persons'. The definition and treatment of refugees is a growing challenge for development, with the number projected to increase due to climate change, growing religious extremism, and the closing of other avenues for migration.

The number of refugees greatly exceeds the number of resettlement slots managed by the UNHRC. Refugees can apply directly for asylum but the vast majority of asylum applications take years to be resolved and are turned down. As a result refugees suffer uncertainty and insecurity and are unable to return home or settle permanently in a new country. They are vulnerable to policy changes that place them at risk of destitution, arrest, or involuntary repatriation and may be confined in camps or holding areas near volatile borders, exposing them to renewed violence. They are often housed in remote locations and are dependent on governments or charities for shelter and to meet basic needs, with meagre education or employment opportunities. Where they are denied freedom of movement and have few economic opportunities to make a living, it is not surprising that refugees become increasingly desperate and are victims of crime, smuggling, and other abuses. As the Palestinian refugees attest, refugees may be stuck in limbo for generations.

Threats to human security are diverse and can stem from armed conflict and civil war as well as from human trafficking and modern forms of slavery, and other gross violations of human rights. *Genocide*—the systematic persecution and extermination of all, or a large part, of a particular group of people along ethnic, racial, religious, or national lines—is the horrifying antithesis of development. The most well-known example of genocide in modern history was the Holocaust which led to the deaths of an estimated 6 million Jews at the hands of the Nazis during the Second World War. Other horrifying cases include the 1994 Rwandan genocide which involved the slaughter of 800,000 Tutsi and others over a hundred-day period by the Hutu majority, and the 1992–5 Bosnian genocide during which 200,000 Muslim civilians were murdered and 2 million more became refugees.

Table 5. Estimates of genocide since the Second World War and associated refugees

Genocide	Date	Estimated number of murders	Estimated number of refugees/displaced
Bangladesh	1971	500,000–3,000,000	—
Cambodia	1975–9	~ 1,700,000	—
East Timor	1975–99	~ 200,000	—
Guatemala	1981–3	~ 200,000	—
Bosnia	1992–5	> 200,000	~ 4,000,000
Rwanda	1994	~ 800,000	~ 2,000,000
Darfur, Sudan	2003 onwards	~ 500,000	~ 3,000,000
Syria*	2011 onwards	> 2,762	+ 4,200,000

Note: Published estimates vary widely according to the source consulted.

* Syria is not widely recognized as a case of genocide yet, although an alert has been issued by Genocide Watch. The number of deaths due to genocide reported for Syria is an underestimate. It includes 1,400 plus people gassed by the Assad regime in 2013, and 1,362 civilians murdered by ISIS between June 2014 and April 2015. Other groups in the region may also be responsible for genocide, although no reliable statistics are available. The number of Syrian refugees reported in this table is dwarfed by the 7.6 million forced relocations and the 12.2 million people in critical need of humanitarian assistance. Distinguishing between deaths related to conflict and deaths related to genocide is not easy. The latter is confined to acts intended to destroy or persecute a specific ethnic or religious group.

Source: Scott Lamb, 'Genocide since 1945: Never Again?' *Spiegel Online.* http://www.spiegel.de/international/genocide-since-1945-never-again-a-338612.html (last accessed 31 March 2015); the estimated number of murders for Darfur is from Eric Reeves, 'Abandoning the Victims of Genocide in Darfur', *The WorldPost* online (2015), http://www.huffingtonpost.com/eric-reeves/abandoning-the-victims-of-genocide-in-darfur_b_7486878.html (last accessed 5 July 2015); the estimate of the number of refugees are from WWG (2015), 'Genocides and Conflict', *World Without Genocide,* http://worldwithoutgenocide.org/genocides-and-conflicts (last accessed 11 October 2015); the figures for Syria are from Genocide Watch, 'Genocide Alert: The Syrian Arab Republic' (August 2015), http://genocidewatch.net/2015/08/20/genocide-watch-alert-2015-on-syria/ (last accessed 11 October 2015) and United to End Genocide, 'Syria Backgrounder', http://endgenocide.org/conflict-areas/syria-backgrounder/ (last accessed 11 October 2015).

Genocide is more common than is often realized. Despite the resolve to never repeat the crimes of the 1915 Armenian genocide or the Holocaust following the Second World War, the second half of the twentieth century and the beginning of the twenty-first century have been punctuated with several other tragic examples of genocide. Although the details are often difficult to ascertain, these travesties of human rights and development account for an estimated 5 million murders and many more forced relocations (Table 5).

Genocide is illegal under international law (the United Nations adopted a resolution affirming that genocide is illegal in 1948) but it was only with the development of the international criminal court in the 1990s that the international community has had the mandate to act under the United Nations umbrella to prevent genocide. The concept of the 'responsibility to protect' has also been associated with the development of a framework to overcome the historical aversion of the United Nations to interfere in the domestic activities of member nations. Despite the development of a framework, the international community continues to fail in preventing genocide and systematic attacks on civilians, as events in Syria and elsewhere attest.

The establishment of global security and the implementation of agreements which seek to prevent genocide and facilitate the safe movement and fair treatment of migrants and refugees is a key responsibility of the international community. Achieving this aim has a direct bearing on development.

8

⊗⊗⊗

The Future of Development

Over the past seventy-five years ideas about the responsibility of development have shifted from the colonial and patronizing view that poor countries were incapable of developing on their own and required the guidance and help of the rich colonial powers to a view that each country has a primary responsibility over its own development aims and outcomes and that development cannot be imposed from outside. However, while both colonial and Marxist ideas of the interplay of advanced and developing countries are discredited, foreign powers and the international community can still exercise a profound impact on development—for better or for worse. This goes well beyond development aid as international trade, investment, security, environmental, and other policies are typically more important. The quantity and quality of aid, the type of aid, as well as its predictability and alignment with national objectives nevertheless can play a vital role in contributing to development outcomes, particularly for low-income countries and the least developed economies. Access to appropriate technologies and capacity building helps to lay the foundation for improved livelihoods. So although development must be done by countries and citizens themselves, the extent to which the international community is facilitating or frustrating development continues to influence and at times even dramatically shape development trajectories.

The extraordinary progress made in poverty reduction is evidence that development does happen. As is evident in Figure 12, the number of people living under $1.90 a day (at 2011 PPP) fell by just over one billion between 1990 and 2012, even though the population of developing countries increased by more than 2 billion over the same period. Much of this decline is attributable to the progress made in China, and to a lesser extent East Asia and India. The greatest development challenge remains in sub-Saharan Africa. We showed earlier that, particularly for the poorest countries, aid remains central to development efforts, but that aid also plays a vital role in middle-income and even richer countries in addressing public goods.

The latest poverty estimates for 2015 point to a further reduction in the number of people living below the $1.90 poverty line, to around 702 million, the vast majority of whom continue to be located in South Asia and sub-Saharan Africa (Table 6). By 2030 the number of people living below the $1.90 poverty line is projected to almost halve again (to around 411 million), with the vast majority of gains being

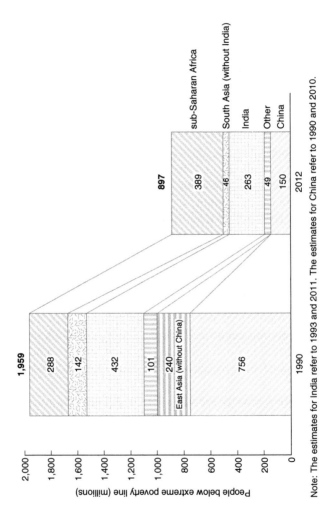

Note: The estimates for India refer to 1993 and 2011. The estimates for China refer to 1990 and 2010.

Figure 12 People living on less than $1.90 per day by region (1990–2012).

Table 6. Total number and proportion of people below the $1.90 poverty line (1990–2015)

	Proportion below $1.90 per day PPP 2011				Millions of people below $1.90 a day PPP 2011			
	1990	1999	2012	2015	1990	1999	2012	2015
East Asia & Pacific	60.6	37.5	7.2	4.1	995.5	689.4	147.2	82.6
Europe & Central Asia	1.9	7.8	2.1	1.7	8.8	36.8	10.1	4.4
Latin America & the Caribbean	17.8	13.9	5.6	5.6	78.2	71.1	33.7	29.7
South Asia	50.6	—	18.8	13.5	574.6	—	309.2	231.3
Sub-Saharan Africa	56.8	58.0	42.7	35.2	287.6	374.6	388.8	347.1
World	37.1	29.1	12.7	9.6	1958.6	1751.5	896.7	702.1

Note: The Middle East and North Africa (MENA) is omitted as survey data coverage is too low. The available evidence implies a poverty rate of 2.3% in the MENA region in 2012 and a poverty rate of 41.2% for South Asia in 1999. 2015 = projection.

Source: PovcalNet: The Online Tool For Poverty Measurement (Development Research Group, World Bank), http://iresearch.worldbank.org/PovcalNet/index.htm?1 (last accessed 18 October 2015); the figures for 2015 are taken from Marcio Cruz, James Foster, Bryce Quillin, and Philip Schellekens, 'Ending Extreme Poverty and Sharing Prosperity: Progress and Policies', *Policy Research Note* (World Bank, 2015), p. 6 and Table 1.

made in South Asia where 286 million people are expected to escape extreme poverty.

It is now widely recognized that while governments must set the stage and invest in infrastructure, health, education, and other public goods, the private sector is the engine of growth and job creation.

A key challenge for all countries is the *sequencing* of different policy reforms and investment efforts. Given the wide array of pressing needs facing governments in developing countries, and limited financial and institutional capacity, tough choices need to be made as to what should come first. Shortfalls in funding, personnel, equipment, and other capacity constraints mean that not everyone can be provided with even the most basic of needs, such as clean water, sanitation, electricity, roads, education, and health at the same time. Nor can all regions within a country be catered for simultaneously.

Communities are acutely aware of these constraints, and approaches which involve citizens in the choices of what and how basic services should be provided typically yield the greatest development impact. Investments and reforms that generate skills and facilitate private sector development lay the ground for future employment and tax revenues and allow more to be achieved over time. Infrastructure, including the provision of water and sanitation, reliable supplies of electricity, and transport systems provide an essential foundation for development. The provision of universal basic education and health is essential. Policies that improve governance and reduce corruption and that raise standards of education and skills encourage employment.

Whereas in early stages of development and times of crisis, foreign borrowing and aid may be required to supplement domestic revenues, it is essential that governments raise their revenues as well as expenditures to ensure that their growth may be sustained without resort to risky levels of debt.

The distributional consequences of sequencing decisions have a powerful effect on development outcomes. In too many countries, the wealthy dwellers of the capital cities use their connections to power to ensure that their needs are attended to before those of the poor. This tends to skew investments towards the wealthier areas of major cities and reinforces growing inequality in societies. Widening access to basic services, such as primary education and health, electricity and water, with tariff and charging structures reflecting the ability to pay, allows for broader-based development, within any budget envelope.

The role and sequencing of private investment and foreign aid is another important consideration. Private investment is vital and the prior establishment of transparent and accountable laws and regulations which include safeguards regarding the health and safety of workers, the control of pollution, and ensuring respect for ownership rights and good governance, encourages the growth of a thriving private sector which advances development. In resource-rich countries, the lessons of the many past failures need to be learnt in order to avoid the resource curse which too often has been associated with predatory investments in natural resources. Ensuring that revenues from mining and other natural resources benefit the many and are not captured by the few is essential, with sovereign wealth funds and other mechanisms offering a means to reduce the risk.

The *coherence* of aid and other policies is an important consideration. For example, as we saw in the preceding chapters, supporting agricultural systems in developing countries requires not only investments in rural roads and irrigation, but also support for international research which will provide improved seeds, trade reform which allows access to crops, and actions which will stop the devastating impact of climate change on agricultural systems in many of the poorest countries. As noted earlier, the establishment of a level playing field for trade, and in particular the reduction of the agricultural subsidies and tariff and non-tariff barriers in rich countries that severely discriminates against agricultural development and increase food price instability, would provide a greater impetus for many developing countries than aid. Not all trade is good, and the prevention of small arms trade, toxic waste, slave and sex trafficking, and other illicit trade should be curtailed and corruption dealt with decisively. The prevention of transfer pricing and of tax avoidance is important in building a sound revenue base which provides the means for governments to invest in infrastructure and health, education, and other systems which provide the foundation for development.

The relationship between investments in energy and the need to reduce carbon emissions to restrict global warming is a vital area where greater coherence is required. Reducing carbon emissions requires that developing countries be helped to invest in non-carbon energy sources. This requires very significant increases in support for the financing of renewables and other non-carbon energy sources as well as technological transfers and support for capacity building in order to ensure that developing countries can climb the steep energy curve required to provide for their people's needs. We face two great challenges: the eradication of poverty and slowing climate change. Ensuring the coherence of our actions in achieving these two vital challenges is essential.

The provision of *global public goods* is as essential as development assistance to individual countries. Such measures can for example improve the availability, price, and effectiveness of vaccinations and drugs, especially against tropical diseases and the treatment of HIV/AIDS. The creation of an intellectual property regime that allows for affordable drugs and the encouragement of research on drugs and technologies that foster development, not least in agriculture, is another essential role for the international community.

The international community has a central role to play in the protection and restoration of the global commons, not least with respect to climate change and the environment. The establishment of global security and the implementation of agreements which seek to prevent genocide and facilitate the safe movement and fair treatment of migrants and refugees is another key responsibility of the international community. So too is the prevention of systemic risks. Poor people and poor countries are most vulnerable to all forms of risk, and international efforts to reduce systemic risks which cascade over national borders is another area which requires the coming together of the international community.

Development is a national responsibility, but in an increasingly integrated world the international community has a greater responsibility to help manage the global commons as an increasing share of problems spill over national borders. All countries of the world share a collective responsibility for the planet, but the bigger and more advanced the country, the larger the share of this responsibility that it is capable of shouldering.

Our Common Future

As individuals get wealthier and escape poverty the choices they make increasingly impact others. The tension between individual choice and collective outcomes is not new, with the study of the management of *commons* going back at least five hundred years. Commons were shared lands, rivers, or other natural resources over which citizens had access. In England, the rights of access became defined in *common law*. Many of these rights were removed in the enclosure movement which in the eighteen century converted most of the common lands into private property.

The *tragedy of the commons* refers to the overexploitation of common resources. Early examples include the overfishing of rivers, overgrazing of village fields, or depletion of underground water. The management of the commons has led to the development of customary and more recently legally enforceable rules and regulations which limit the exploitation of shared resources. In recent decades however, the pressure on common resources, and in particular on the *global commons*, has grown with population and incomes.

The global commons refers to the earth's shared natural resources, and includes the oceans, atmosphere, polar regions, and outer space.

Development has meant that we are moving from a world of barely 500 million middle-class consumers in the 1980s to a world of over 4 billion middle-class consumers in the coming decade. This triumph of development is a cause for celebration. But it provides a source for growing alarm over our ability to cooperate and coexist in a sustainable manner on our beautiful planet. Greater individual choice is for many regarded as a key objective and outcome of development processes. Other outcomes include increasing life expectancy, higher incomes, and rising consumption. Development has resulted in rapid population growth—2 billion more people over the past twenty-five years with a further 2 billion plus expected by 2050 (Table 2). And globalization has seen not only more connectivity but also an increase in the global flows of goods and services, with the sourcing of products and services from more distant places. The pressure on scarce resources has never been greater. Nor has the difficulty of managing them.

The result is a sharp rise in the challenge of managing the global commons, coupled with the rise of new collective challenges. Antibiotic resistance is one of these new challenges. While it is rational for individuals to take antibiotics to defeat infections, the more that people take antibiotics, the higher the risk of resistance. When combined with the growing use of antibiotics in animals—which now consume 80 per cent of antibiotics worldwide—there is an escalating risk of antibiotic resistance. This would lead to rapid declines in the effectiveness of antibiotics, with dramatically negative consequences on these essential components of modern medicine. Other examples of the tension between our individual choice and collective outcomes include the consumption of tuna and other fish which are threatened with extinction, or our individual use of fossil-fuel energy and the resulting collective implications for climate change.

As development raises income and consumption and increases connectivity, the spillover impact of individual actions grows. Many of these spillovers are positive. Evidence includes the close correlation between urbanization and development. When people come together they can do things that they could never achieve on their own. However as incomes rise, so too do the often unintended negative spillover effects, with examples including obesity, climate change, antibiotic resistance, and biodiversity loss. Rising inequality and the erosion of social cohesion are also growing risks.

As Sen identified, a key objective of development is freedom. Freedom to avoid want and starvation, to overcome insecurity and discrimination, and above all to be capable of achieving those things we have reason to value. But with this freedom comes new responsibilities. Our individual contribution to our shared outcomes and as guardians of future generations rises with our own development. If development is to be realized for all people, now and in the future, it is vital that we too develop as individuals. We need to ensure that we are free of the ignorance of how our actions interact with others. *Development brings new responsibilities as well as freedoms.*

Ideas for Development

This book has shown that there is no simple recipe for development. The pursuit of development is necessarily shaped by a combination of history and geography. But history is not destiny, as illustrated by the extraordinary range of outcomes of countries with rather similar pasts and comparable geographical positions.

Growth is an important but inadequate objective. Resource-rich Angola has for many years been amongst the fastest growing countries in Africa and the world, but it remains amongst the most stubbornly poor performers on most development indicators as the benefits of growth have been captured by a small elite. Meanwhile, its neighbour Botswana, although well endowed with diamonds, has escaped the resource curse and seen much of its population escape poverty through better governance. A Cuban may expect to live anywhere between four and sixteen years longer than citizens on the neighbouring islands of Barbados, Dominican Republic, and Haiti, and Cubans even have higher life expectancy than the USA, where people are on average almost ten times richer.

The worldwide progress in recent decades has been remarkable. Development happens, as people and societies throw off old ideas and take on new, better ideas. Ideas that allow people to escape poverty and lead longer and healthier lives, ideas that combine an understanding of economic and social change which embraces all of society, regardless of gender, age, disability, creed, race, or sexual preferences. In recent decades, access to ideas has leapfrogged, as Internet access has increased the advantages of literacy and connectivity. But not only good ideas spread more rapidly. So too do bad ideas, such as those propagated by Islamic State (ISIS) and other extremist movements. As the battle of ideas has become global, it has become even more important to ensure that those ideas which promote development are more widely disseminated and that individuals in all societies, and not least the youth, embrace the hope of development.

Development is about learning. Learning what works and what does not, where and why. This requires a dissection of not only successes but also failures. Leaders, aid agencies, and experts too often trumpet their purported achievements and bury the vital lessons from failures. There are many factors that are significant in the pursuit of development, but openness and accountability, where leaders listen to the insights of citizens and draw inspiration from their past experience and that of others, is a vital ingredient of sustained progress. So too is the integration of long-term perspectives and goals, to ensure that the benefits of development are sustained for decades to come, reducing the risks associated with resource depletion, climate change, and the growing range of potentially disastrous consequences of short-sighted growth which fundamentally threatens the continued pursuit of development.

Make Poverty History

In rich and poor countries alike, development has never been the preserve of governments alone. In recent decades, the number of citizens and businesses engaged in questions of development has grown rapidly. Thousands of international NGOs are involved in grass-roots campaigns to raise awareness, raise funds, influence policy, and build solidarity to achieve wide-ranging development objectives.

Awareness has been raised through music, social media, and the association of iconic individuals and brands with campaigns which highlight development concerns. In 1971, the former Beatle George Harrison together with Ravi Shankar organized a groundbreaking benefit concert and produced a record to raise awareness and funds for victims of the Bangladesh genocide. In 1984, Bob Geldof formed Band Aid and together with leading musicians performed at Live Aid concerts in support of victims of the Ethiopian Famine. Subsequently, a growing number of musicians and actors have been associated with a wide range of public causes. In the 1980s songs and concerts supported the anti-apartheid struggle and the release of Nelson Mandela.

In 2005, the Make Poverty History campaign raised the pressure on attendees at the Gleneagles 2005 G8 Summit to increase aid commitments and adhere to the Millennium Development Goals. In 2007, Live Earth served to raise awareness of climate change. In its annual Red Nose Day and Sports Relief events, Comic Relief has involved celebrities to raise awareness, engaging citizens who may otherwise not been aware of development objectives and encouraging them to support local and international development causes. The role of celebrities in raising awareness has been formalized by organizations such as the United Nations International Children's Emergency Fund (UNICEF) which has established a partnership with the Barcelona Football Club and appointed celebrity ambassadors, including David Beckham and Andy Murray. UNHCR similarly has appointed Angelina Jolie as its Special Envoy to raise awareness of the plight of refugees. Meanwhile, Bono has been active for decades on development and associated issues, including through a dedicated campaigning organization ONE.

While a positive vision for the need for development is gaining traction, so too are the threats which arise out of growing interdependency. The tragedy of the destruction of the World Trade Centre on September 11th 2001 and the subsequent attack on Afghanistan by the United States demonstrated that what happens in the poorest countries in the world can dramatically impact lives in the richest places on the planet. More recently, the growth of fundamentalism in the Middle East has highlighted the risks associated with failures of development in that region. Pandemics also pose a rising risk; with the great hub airports connecting worldwide travellers, it is estimated that a pandemic could become global within 48 hours. Cyber attacks point to the potential for instantaneous disruption and add a new dimension to systemic risks which transcend national borders.

As the flow of ideas, people, products, and services across borders grows, facilitated by the Internet and other technological advances and social media, so too does our awareness of our common humanity. We live in an era when for the first time in history we can realistically imagine and achieve in our lifetimes a world free of poverty and many of the diseases that have afflicted humanity for millennia. Remarkably, eradicating poverty has been agreed globally as SDG1. Recent decades have demonstrated that development does happen and does change lives. While there is no replicable silver bullet to achieve this, our understanding of development has evolved both conceptually and practically to provide an increasingly effective toolbox which is widely applicable.

In this volume I have pointed to some of the key lessons learnt and the opportunities these provide for societies to advance. The prospects for advancement have never been greater. But the risks are also rising, and development could be stunted or set back. Globalization is simultaneously a source of the greatest opportunity and also the source of new systemic risks that will impact on all our futures.

All of our futures are intertwined with the future of developing countries. Extraordinary creativity and opportunity will emerge from developing countries. We can look forward to the flourishing of modern Einsteins, Shakespeares, and other creative geniuses as over five billion literate and increasingly educated people begin to contribute to global development. At the same time, we should be aware that we are dealing with the biggest challenges in our lives, such as climate change, conflict, fundamentalism, and pandemics. This will require increasing cooperation and partnership. More than ever the futures of advanced and developing countries are intertwined. Indeed, the term 'development' is less and less about a geographic place and more and more about our collective ability to cooperate in harvesting global opportunities and managing the associated global risks. Development is not simply or mainly about the lives of others. It is about ourselves and what we care about. Development is about who we are and our collective future.

SOURCES FOR FIGURES AND BOXES

FIGURES

1. Maddison Project Database (2013 version), http://www. ggdc.net/maddison/maddison-project/home.htm (last accessed 3 August 2015). The data in the graph refers to constant GDP per capita in 1990 International Geary-Khamis dollars.

2. Maddison Project Database (2013 version), http://www. ggdc.net/maddison/maddison-project/home.htm (last accessed 3 August 2015). The data in the graph refers to constant GDP per capita in 1990 International Geary-Khamis dollars.

3. Author.

4. Adapted from Amar Bhattacharya, Mattia Romani, and Nicholas Stern, 'Infrastructure for Development: Meeting the Challenge', Policy Paper, Centre for Climate Change Economics and Policy (Grantham Research Institute on Climate Change and the Environment, 2012), p. 13. Reproduced by permission of the authors.

5. Compiled from *UCDP/PRIO Armed Conflict Dataset v.4-2015, 1946–2014*, Uppsala Conflict Data Program, http://www.pcr.uu.se/research/ucdp/datasets/ucdp_prio_armed_conflict_dataset/ (last accessed July 2015).

6. Author's calculation and World Bank, *World Development Indicators*, http://data.worldbank.org/ (last accessed 4 October 2015).

7. Compiled from OECD Stat, http://stats.oecd.org/ (22 October 2015).

8. Author's calculation and World Bank, *World Development Indicators* (online), http://data.worldbank.org/ (last accessed 24 September 2015). Data for remittances for 2013–15 is taken from World Bank, 'Migration and Remittances: Recent Developments and Outlook', *Migration and Development Brief 24* (13 April 2015), p. 4, http://siteresources.worldbank.org/INTPROSPECTS/Resources/334934-1288990760745/MigrationandDevelopmentBrief24.pdf (last accessed 30 September 2015). Data for foreign direct investment for 2012–15 is taken from UNCTAD, 'Global FDI Flows Declined in 2014', *Global Investment Trends Monitor 18* (United Nations, 29 January 2015), p. 7, http://unctad.org/en/PublicationsLibrary/ webdiaeia2015d1_en.pdf (last accessed 30 September 2015).

9. OECD Stat, http://stats.oecd.org/ (July 2015); and for the BRICS, author's calculations based on the following sources: OECD, 'Table 33a. Estimates of concessional finance for development (ODA-like flows) of key providers of development co-operation that do not report

to the OECD-DAC: Brazil, Chile, China, Colombia, India, Indonesia, Mexico, Qatar, South Africa', http://www.oecd. org/dac/stats/statisticsonresourceflowstodevelopingcountries. htm (last accessed 14 May 2015); and Russian Government, *The Russian Federation ODA: National Report*, p. 1, http:// www.minfin.ru/common/img/uploaded/library/2012/05/ PresentationEng2012-0.pdf (last accessed 3 August 2015); in addition, the 2006 statistics for Brazil, India, China, and South Africa are from United Nations, *Trends in South-South and Triangular Development Cooperation*, Background Study for the Development Cooperation Forum (United Nations Economic and Social Council, April 2008), Table 2, p. 12; the 2010 statistic for Brazil is from IPEA, *Brazilian Cooperation for International Development 2010* (Institute for Applied Economic Research, 2014), p. 5; and the 2012 and 2013 statistics for Brazil are informed guesstimates ($1 billion for both years) based on the previous source and Lídia Cabral and Julia Weinstock, 'Brazil: An Emerging Aid Player', *ODI Briefing Paper 64* (Overseas Development Institute, 2010), p. 1.

10. OECD Stat, http://stats.oecd.org/ (July 2015); and for the BRICS, author's calculations based on the following sources: OECD, 'Table 33a. Estimates of concessional finance for development (ODA-like flows) of key providers of development co-operation that do not report to the OECD-DAC: Brazil, Chile, China, Colombia, India, Indonesia, Mexico, Qatar, South Africa', http://www.oecd.org/ dac/stats/statisticsonresourceflowstodevelopingcountries. htm (last accessed 14 May 2015); and Russian Government,

The Russian Federation ODA: National Report, p. 1, http://
www.minfin.ru/common/img/uploaded/library/2012/
05/ PresentationEng2012-0.pdf (last accessed 3 August
2015); in addition, the 2006 statistics for Brazil, India,
China, and South Africa are from United Nations, *Trends
in South-South and Triangular Development Cooperation*,
Background Study for the Development Cooperation
Forum (United Nations Economic and Social Council,
April 2008), Table 2, p. 12; the 2010 statistic for Brazil is
from IPEA, *Brazilian Cooperation for International Development 2010* (Institute for Applied Economic Research,
2014), p. 5; and the 2012 and 2013 statistics for Brazil
are informed guesstimates ($1 billion for both years)
based on the previous source and Lídia Cabral and Julia
Weinstock, 'Brazil: An Emerging Aid Player', *ODI Briefing
Paper 64* (Overseas Development Institute, 2010), p. 1.

11. Author's calculation based on statistics from *WIPO IP
Statistics Data Centre* (last updated March 2015), http://
ipstats.wipo.int/ipstatv2/, The World Intellectual Property
Organization (WIPO) (last accessed 7 October 2015).

12. Based on statistics from *PovcalNet: The Online Tool For
Poverty Measurement* (Development Research Group,
World Bank), http://iresearch.worldbank.org/PovcalNet/
index.htm?1 (accessed 18 October 2015).

BOXES

1. Author.

2. H. Myint, 'Economic Theory and Development Policy', *Economica*, 34 (134) (1967): 117–30.

3. United Nations, 'Official List of MDG Indicators' (2008), http://mdgs.un.org/unsd/mdg/Host.aspx?Content=Indi cators/OfficialList.htm (last accessed 3 August 2015).

4. United Nations, 'SustainableDevelopment Goals (SDGs)', http://www.undp.org/content/undp/en/home/mdgoverview/ post-2015-development-agenda.html (last accessed 5 October 2015).

REFERENCES

CHAPTER 1: WHAT IS DEVELOPMENT?

Development patterns across countries: The analysis of long-term growth for Argentina, Ghana and South Korea utilizes available data on GDP per capita in 1990 US$ from the Maddison Project Database, http://www.ggdc.net/maddison/maddison-project/home.htm (2013 version) (last accessed 3 August 2015); the other statistics are from *World Development Indicators*, http://data.worldbank.org/ (last accessed 18 October 2015). The per capita income figures refer to current US dollars; see also Ha-Joon Chang, *Economics: The User's Guide—A Pelican Introduction* (Pelican, 2014) on Equatorial Guinea; and Jean Drèze and Amartya Sen, *An Uncertain Glory: India and Its Contradictions* (Princeton University Press, 2013), statistical annex for Kerala.

Development, n.: *Oxford English Dictionary Online* (Oxford University Press, 2014).

Progress of opulence: Adam Smith, *An Inquiry into the Nature and Causes of The Wealth of Nations* (Chicago University Press, [1776] 1976).

'Opportunity for a full life' and 'realization of human personality' quotations: Paul Streeten, 'The Meaning and Measurement of Development' in A. K. Dutt and J. Ros (eds), *International Handbook of Development Economics: Volume 1* (Edward Elgar, 2008), pp. 3–15; and Dudley Seers, 'What Are We Trying to Measure?' *Journal of Development Studies*, 8 (3) (1972): 21–36.

How to measure development: World Bank's 'Data Catalog' and description of indicators, http://data.worldbank.org/; Moshe Syrquin 'Structural Transformation' in D. A. Clark (ed.), *The Elgar Companion to Development Studies* (Edward Elgar, 2006), pp. 601–7; Tim Beasley and Louis Cord, *Delivering on the Promise of Pro-Poor Growth: Insights and Lessons from Country Experiences* (World Bank Publications, 2006); Diane Coyle, *GDP: A Brief But Affectionate History* (Princeton University Press, 2014); and World Bank, *The East Asian Miracle: Economic Growth and Public Policy* (Oxford University Press, 1993).

Measure of Economic Welfare: William Nordhaus and James Tobin, *Is Growth Obsolete?* (National Bureau of Economic Research, 1972).

Beyond growth (redistribution and basic needs): Paul Streeten, 'From Growth to Basic Needs', *Finance and Development*, 16 (1) (1979): 39–42; Hollis Chenery, Montek Ahluwalia, C. L. G. Bell, John Duloy, and Richard Jolly, *Redistribution with Growth* (Oxford University Press, 1974); and ILO, *Employment, Growth and Basic Needs: A One World Problem* (International Labour Organization, 1976).

ILO 'prosperity quote': ILO, 'Declaration of Philadelphia' (International Labour Organization, 1944).

Human development: UNDP, *Human Development Report 1996: Economics Growth and Human Development* (Oxford University Press, 1996).

Participatory Development: Robert Chambers, *Whose Reality Counts? Putting the First Last* (ITDG, 1997).

Development as capability expansion and freedom: Amartya K. Sen, *Development as Freedom* (Oxford University Press, 1999).

Development Goals: Howard White, 'Millennium Development Goals' in D. A. Clark (ed.), *The Elgar Companion to Development Studies* (Edward Elgar, 2006), pp. 382–9; see also the references to

David Hulme and the Sustainable Development Goals Knowledge Platform in Chapter 5.

Development Dashboards: OECD, 'Better Life Index', http://www.oecdbetterlifeindex.org/ (last accessed 1 August 2015); John Helliwell, Richard Layard, and Jeffrey Sachs (eds), *World Happiness Report 2012*, http://worldhappiness.report/ed/2012/ (last accessed 1 August 2015); and Joseph Stiglitz, Amartya Sen, and Jean-Paul Fitoussi, *Mis-measuring Our Lives: Why GDP Doesn't Add Up* (New Press, 2010).

Subjective well-being and new measures: David A. Clark 'Defining and Measuring Human Well-Being' in B. Freeman (ed.), *Global Environmental Change: Handbook of Global Environmental Pollution* (Springer, 2014), pp. 833–55.

CHAPTER 2: HOW DOES DEVELOPMENT HAPPEN?

Classical political economy and development: Adam Smith, 'An Inquiry into the Nature and the Causes of the Wealth of Nations' [1776], reprinted in E. Cannon (ed.), *The Wealth of Nations* (University of Chicago Press, 1976); David Ricardo, *On the Principles of Political Economy, and Taxation* (John Murray, 1817); Thomas Malthus, *Principles of Political Economy* (J. Johnson, 1820); Karl Marx, 'Preface' in *A Contribution to The Critique of Political Economy* (Progress Publishers, 1858); Karl Marx and Friedrich Engels, 'The Manifesto of the Communist Party' in *Marx/Engels Selected Works*, Vol. 1 (Progress Publishers, 1969): 98–137; and John Stuart Mill, *Principles of Political Economy*, 7th edition (Longmans, Green and Co. [1820] 1909).

Modernization theory: Andrew Webster, *Introduction to Sociology of Development* (Macmillan, 1991), chapter 3.

Planning for development (including big push theory, the stages of growth, and unbalanced growth): Paul Rosenstein-Rodan, 'Problems of Industrialisation of Eastern and South-Eastern Europe',

The Economic Journal, 53 (210/211): 202–11; Ragnar Nurkse, *Problems of Capital Formation in Underdeveloped Countries* (Blackwell, 1953); W. Arthur Lewis, 'Economic Development with Unlimited Supplies of Labour', *The Manchester School*, 22 (2) (1954): 139–91; Walt Rostow, *The Stages of Economic Growth: A Non-Communist Manifesto* (Cambridge University Press, 1960); and Albert Hirschman, *The Strategy of Economic Development* (Yale University Press, 1958).

Dependency theory and the Singer–Prebisch hypothesis: Hans Singer, 'Economic Progress in Underdeveloped Countries', *Social Research: An International Quarterly of Political and Social Science*, 16 (1) (1949): 1–11; Raúl Prebisch, *ECLAC Manifesto* (ECLAC, 1949); and Gabriel Palma, 'Dependency: A Formal Theory of Underdevelopment or a Methodology for the Analysis of Concrete Situations of Underdevelopment?' *World Development*, 6 (7–8), (1978): 881–924.

Neo-Classical Market-led Development, 'getting the prices rights', and rent seeking: Anne Krueger, 'The Political Economy of the Rent Seeking Society', *American Economic Review*, 64 (3) (1974): 291–303; and Deepak Lal, *The Poverty of Development Economics* (Harvard University Press, 1985); on African countries adopting the Neo-Classical approach see Thandika Mkandawire and Charles Soludo, *Our Continent, Our Future: African Perspectives on Structural Adjustment* (Africa World Press, 1998).

CHAPTER 3: WHY ARE SOME COUNTRIES RICH AND OTHERS POOR?

Statistics on convergent and divergent growth across regions and countries: Analysis of long-term growth (1870–2010) utilizes available data on GDP per capita in 1990 US$ from the Maddison Project Database, http://www.ggdc.net/maddison/maddison-project/home.htm (2013 version); the analysis of divergent growth patterns for the period 1960–2014 (including statistics for Ghana, South Korea, and China) draws on available data on GDP per capita in 2005 US$ from the World Bank, *World Development Indicators (online)*, http://data.worldbank.org/ (last accessed 29 September 2015).

Uneven development and convergence: Robert Solow, 'A Contribution to the Theory of Economic Growth', *The Quarterly Journal of Economics* 70 (1) (1956): 65–94; William Baumol, 'Productivity Growth, Convergence and Welfare: What the Long-Run Data Says', *American Economic Review*, 76 (1986): 1072–85; Stephen Parente and Edward Prescott, 'Changes in the Wealth of Nations', *Quarterly Review*, 17 (2) (1993): 3–16; and Haizheng Li and Zhenhui Xu, 'Economic Convergence in Seven Asian Economies', *Review of Development Economics*, 11 (3) (2007): 531–49.

South East Asian Miracle: Ajit Singh, '"Close" vs. "Strategic" Integration with the World Economy and the "Market Friendly Approach to Development" vs. "An Industrial Policy"', MPRA Paper No. 53562 (8 February, 1995), https://mpra.ub.uni-muenchen.de/53562/1/MPRA_paper_53562.pdf (last accessed 1 October 2015); and John Page, 'The East Asian Miracle: Four Lessons for Development Policy' in S. Fischer and J. Rotemberg (eds), *NBER Macroeconomics Manual 1994* (MIT, 1994), pp. 219–82, http://www.nber.org/chapters/c11011.pdf (last accessed 1 October 2015).

Poverty and inequality: *PovcalNet: The Online Tool For Poverty Measurement* (Development Research Group, World Bank), http://iresearch.worldbank.org/PovcalNet/index.htm?1 (last accessed 18 October 2015); Marcio Cruz, James Foster, Bryce Quillin, and Philip Schellekens, 'Ending Extreme Poverty and Sharing Prosperity: Progress and Policies', *Policy Research Note* (World Bank, 2015), p. 6 and Table 1; Anap Shah, 'Poverty Facts and Stats', *Global Issues*, http://www.globalissues.org/article/26/poverty-facts-and-stats#src2 (last accessed 10 October 2015); and Andy Sumner, 'Global Poverty and the New Bottom Billion', Working Paper (Institute of Development Studies, 12 September 2010), https://www.ids.ac.uk/files/dmfile/GlobalPovertyDataPaper1.pdf (last accessed 10 October 2015).

Resource endowments and the resource curse: Paul Collier, *The Bottom Billion: Why the Poorest Countries Are Failing and What Can Be Done About It* (Oxford University Press, 2008); Jeffrey Frankel, *The Natural Resource Curse* (National Bureau of Economic Research, 2010); and William Easterly and Ross Levine, 'Tropics, Germs and Crops: How Endowments Influence Economic Development', *Journal of Monetary Economics*, 50 (1) (2003): 3–30.

Relationship between trade and development: Jeffrey Sachs and Andrew Warner, *Economic Convergence and Economic Policies* (National Bureau of Economic Research, 1995); and Jeffrey Frankel and David Romer, 'Does Trade Cause Growth?' *American Economic Review*, 89 (3) (1999): 379–99.

Globalization and development: Ian Goldin and Kenneth Reinert, *Globalization for Development: Meeting New Challenges* (Oxford University Press, 2012).

Geographical explanations of development: Jared Diamond, *Guns, Germs and Steel* (Vintage, 1997); and Jeffrey Sachs, *Developing Country Debt and the World Economy* (University of Chicago Press, 1989).

Estimate of deaths from Malaria: WHO, 'WHO/UNICEF Report: Malaria MDG Target Achieved amid Sharp Drop in Cases and Mortality, but 3 Billion People Remain at Risk', Joint WHO/ UNICEF News Release (17 September 2015), http://www.who. int/mediacentre/news/releases/2015/malaria-mdg-target/en/ (last accessed 3 October 2015).

Institutions and governance: Dani Rodrik, Arvind Subramanian, and Francesco Trebbi, 'Institutions Rule: The Primacy of Institutions over Integration and Geography in Economic Development', *Journal of Economic Growth*, 9 (2) (2004): 131–65.

Colonialism and development: Daron Acemoglu, Simon Johnson, and James Robinson, 'The Colonial Origins of Comparative Development: An Empirical Investigation', *American Economic Review*, 91 (5) (2001): 1369–401; and Daron Acemoglu, Simon

Johnson and James Robinson, 'Reversal of Fortune, Geography and Institutions in the Making of the Modern World Income Distribution', *Quarterly Journal of Economics*, 117 (2002): 1231–94.

The role of power and other factors: Amartya Sen, *Poverty and Famines: An Essay on Entitlement and Deprivation* (Clarendon Press, 1981); Colin Bundy, *The Rise and Fall of the South African Peasantry* (Heinemann, 1979); and Jared Diamond, *Guns, Germs and Steel* (Vintage, 1997).

Democracy and development: Irma Adelman, 'Democracy and Development' in D. A. Clark (ed.), *The Elgar Companion to Development Studies* (Edward Elgar, 2006), pp. 105–11; and Daron Acemoglu, Suresh Naidu, Pascual Restrepo, and James Robinson, 'Democracy Does Cause Growth', *NBER Working Paper 200004* (National Bureau of Economic Research, 2014).

Inequality and development: Albert Hirschman, 'The Changing Tolerance for Income Inequality in the Course of Economic Development,' *Quarterly Journal of Economics*, 87 (4) (1973): 544–66; and Simon Kuznets, 'Economic Growth and Income Inequality', *American Economic Review* 45 (1955): 1–28.

CHAPTER 4: WHAT CAN BE DONE TO ACCELERATE DEVELOPMENT?

Demographic transition: Robert Potter, Tony Binns, Jennifer Elliott, and David Smith, *Geographies of Development: An Introduction to Development Studies*, third edition (Pearson Education Ltd, 2008), pp. 197ff.

Gender and development: Nancy Birdsall, 'Gender and Development' in G. Meier (ed.), *Leading Issues in Development Economics*, fifth edition (Oxford University Press, 1995); Joanne Leslie, 'Women's Work and Child Nutrition in the Third World', *World Development*, 16 (11) (1988): 1341–62; Muzi Na, Larissa Jennings,

Sameera Talegawkar, and Saifuddin Ahmed, 'Association between Women's Empowerment and Infant and Child Feeding Practices in sub-Saharan Africa: An Analysis of Demographic and Health Surveys', *Public Health Nutrition* (8 September 2015): http://dx.doi.org/10.1017/S1368980015002621; Anja Tolonen, 'Local Industrial Shocks, Female Empowerment and Infant Health: Evidence from Africa's Gold Mining Industry', Job Market Paper (2015); Jean Drèze and Amartya Sen, *India: Development and Participation* (Oxford University Press, 2002); Amartya Sen, 'Gender and Cooperative Conflicts', in I. Tinker (ed.), *Persistent Inequalities* (Oxford University Press, 1990): pp. 123–49; Grameen Bank, 'Historical Data Series in USD' and 'Past Seventeen Years in USD', http://www.grameen.com (last accessed February 2015); WHO, 'Female Genital Mutilation', Fact Sheet No 241 (World Health Organization, February 2014), http://www.who.int/mediacentre/factsheets/fs241/en/ (last accessed 10 October 2015); and McKinsey & Co, 'How Advancing Women's Equality Can Add $12 Trillion to Global Growth' (September 2015), http://www.mckinsey.com/insights/growth/how_advancing_womens_equality_can_add_12_trillion_to_global_growth (last accessed 4 October 2015).

Education and India: Jean Drèze and Amartya Sen, *An Uncertain Glory: India and Its Contradictions* (Princeton University Press, 2013), chapter 4; and Shailaja Fennell and Madeleine Arnot (eds), *Gender Education and Equality in a Global Context: Conceptual Frameworks and Policy Perspectives* (Routledge, 2009).

Agriculture and development: World Bank, *World Development Report 2008: Agriculture for Development* (World Bank, 2008).

Infrastructure and development: Pravakar Sahooa and Ranjan Dash, 'Economic Growth in South Asia: Role of Infrastructure', *Journal of International Trade and Economic Development*, 21 (2) (2011): 212–52; World Bank, *World Development Report 1990: Poverty* (Oxford University Press, 1990); World Bank, *World Development*

Report 1994: Infrastructure for Development (Oxford University Press, 1994); Amar Bhattacharya, Mattia Romani, and Nicholas Stern, '*Infrastructure for Development: Meeting the Challenge*', Policy Paper, Centre for Climate Change Economics and Policy (Grantham Research Institute on Climate Change and the Environment, 2012).

Legal frameworks and equity: Louis-Alexandre Berg and Deval Desai, *Overview on the Rule of Law and Sustainable Development for the Global Dialogue on Rule of Law and the Post-2015 Development Agenda*, Background Paper (2013); Douglas North, *Institutions, Institutional Change and Economic Performance* (Cambridge University Press, 1990); Amartya Sen, *Development as Freedom* (Oxford University Press, 1999); and Martha Nussbaum, *Women and Human Development: The Capabilities Approach* (Harvard University Press, 2000).

Conflict and life expectancy statistics: Therése Pettersson and Peter Wallensteen, 'Armed Conflicts, 1946–2014', *Journal of Peace Research*, 52 (4) (2015): 536–50; World Bank, *World Development Indicators* (online), http://data.worldbank.org/; and I am Syra, 'Daily Death Toll', http://www.iamsyria.org/daily-death-toll.html (last accessed 4 October 2015).

Conflict and development: World Bank, *World Development Report 2011: Conflict, Security and Development* (World Bank, 2011); Immanuel Kant, *Perpetual Peace* (George Allen and Unwin Ltd, 1795); UN, *An Agenda for Peace*, Report of the Secretary General, A/47/277 (17 June 1992); UN, *Resolution 1366, S/RES/1366* (United Nations Security Council, 30 August 2001); Tom Woodhouse, 'Conflict and Conflict Resolution' in D. A. Clark (ed.), *The Elgar Companion to Development Studies* (Edward Elgar, 2006), pp. 76–81; and Astri Suhrke and Torunn Chaudhary, 'Conflict and Development' in P. A. Haslam, J. Schafer, and P. Beaudet (eds), *Introduction to International Development: Approaches, Actors, and Issues* (Oxford University Press, 2012): 415–36.

CHAPTER 5: THE EVOLUTION OF DEVELOPMENT AID

Primary sources for the whole chapter: Linda Cornwell, 'Aid and Debt' in F. De Beer and H. Swanepoel (eds), *Introduction to Development Studies*, second edition (Oxford University Press, 2000), pp 245–69; and Ian Goldin and Kenneth Reinert, *Globalization for Development: Meeting New Challenges* (Oxford University Press, 2012).

All statistics (unless otherwise stated): World Bank, *World Development Indicators* (online), http://data.worldbank.org/ (last accessed 12 November 2015).

Wasted aid examples: Nicholas Stern, Halsey Rogers, and Ian Goldin, *The Case for Aid* (World Bank, 2002).

Aid effectiveness: DAC, *Shaping the 21st Century* (Development Assistance Committee, OECD, 1996); and David Dollar and Paul Collier, *Aid Allocation and Poverty Reduction* (World Bank, 1999).

Development Goals: David Hulme, 'The Millennium Development Goals (MDGs): A Short History of the World's Biggest Promise', BWPI Working Paper 100 (Brooks World Poverty Institute, 2009); UNDP, 'A New Sustainable Development Agenda', http://www. undp.org/content/undp/en/home/mdgoverview/ (last accessed 5 October 2015); see also the Sustainable Development Knowledge Platform, https://sustainabledevelopment.un.org/sdgsproposal (last accessed 12 November 2015).

Assets of European Investment Bank and China Investment Bank: EIB, *2014 Financial Report* (European Investment Bank, 2014), http://www.eib.org/attachments/general/reports/fr2014en.pdf (last accessed 6 October 2015); and author's estimate based on China Development Bank, 'Performance Highlights', http://www.cdb. com.cn/english/NewsInfo.asp?NewsId=415 (last accessed 6 October 2015).

Aid budgets of biggest bilateral donors: USAID, 'Fiscal Year 2015 Budget Request for Development and Humanitarian Assistance',

Fact Sheet, https://www.usaid.gov/sites/default/files/documents/ 1869/USAIDFY2015DevelopmentBudgetFactSheet.pdf (last accessed 6 October 2015); and DFID, Annual Report and Accounts 2013–14 (Department for International Development, 2014), https://www.gov.uk/government/uploads/system/uploads/attach ment_data/file/331591/annual-report-accounts-2013-14a.pdf (last accessed 6 October 2015).

Capital and assets of financial institutions: World Bank, 'Informa-tion Statement: International Bank of Reconstruction and Devel-opment' (IBRD, 30 June 2014); and author's calculations based on additional figures taken from IDA, 'Management's Discussion & Analysis and Financial Statement, June 2014' (IDA, 2014); IFC, 'Management's Discussion and Analysis and Condensed Consoli-dated Financial Statements December 31, 2014 (Unaudited)' (IFC, 2014); and MIGA, 'Annual Report, 2014' (MIGA, 2014).

Debt crisis and $11 billion outflow from poorest countries: Linda Cornwell, 'Aid and Debt', in F. De Beer and H. Swanepoel (eds), *Introduction to Development Studies*, second edition (Oxford Uni-versity Press, 2000), pp. 245–69.

Debt crisis and response: IMF (2014), 'Debt Relief under the Heavily Indebted Poor Countries (HIPC) Initiative', IMF Factsheet, https://www.imf.org/external/np/exr/facts/hipc.htm (last accessed 30 September 2014); and IMF (2014), 'The Multilateral Debt Relief Initiative', IMF Factsheet, https://www.imf.org/external/ np/exr/facts/mdri.htm (last accessed 30 September 2014).

River blindness and malaria programmes: WHO, 'Prevention of Blindness and Visual Impairment: Onchocerciasis Control Pro-gramme (OCP)' (World Health Organization, 2015), http://www. who.int/blindness/partnerships/onchocerciasis_OCP/en/ (last accessed 12 March 2015). Roll Back Malaria website, http://www. rollbackmalaria.org/ (last accessed 12 November 2015); and UNICEF/WHO, 'Malaria MDG Target Achieved amid Sharp Drop in Cases and Mortality, but 3 Billion People Remain at Risk' (Joint Press Release, 17 September 2015), http://www.rollbackmalaria.

org/files/files/latest_news/press-release-22-sept-2015.pdf (last accessed 5 October 2015).

Building resilience: Ian Goldin and Mike Mariathasan, *The Butterfly Defect: How Globalization Creates Systemic Risk, and What to Do about It* (Princeton University Press, 2014).

Estimate of funds required to mitigate climate change: United Nations Framework Convention on Climate Change News Room, 'Financial Technology and Capacity-Building Support', http://cancun.unfccc.int/financial-technology-and-capacity-building-support/new-long-term-funding-arrangements/ (last accessed 6 October 2015).

International public goods: David Laborde, Will Martin, and Dominique van der Mensbrugghe, 'Implications of the Doha Market Access Proposals for Developing Countries', *World Trade Review*, 11 (1) (2014): 1–25.

Estimated financial cost of SDGs: *The Economist*, '169 Commandments' (28 March 2015).

The future of aid and the contribution of new donors: OECD Stat (online), http://stats.oecd.org/ (last accessed 3 August 2015); OECD, 'Table 33a. Estimates of concessional finance for development (ODA-like flows) of key providers of development co-operation that do not report to the OECD-DAC: Brazil, Chile, China, Colombia, India, Indonesia, Mexico, Qatar, South Africa', http://www.oecd.org/dac/stats/statisticsonresourceflowstodeveloping countries.htm (last accessed 14 May 2015); Comic Relief (2015), 'The Difference We've Made: Facts and Stats', Comic Relief website, http://www.comicrelief.com/how-we-help/the-difference-we-have-made (last accessed 16 March 2015); Hudson Institute (2013), *Index of Global Philanthropy and Remittances 2013: With a Special Report on Emerging Economies* (Hudson Institute, 2013), http://www.idrc.ca/EN/Documents/2013-Global-Philanthropy-Index.pdf; and Gates Foundation, 'Who We Are: Foundation Fact Sheet', http://www.gatesfoundation.org/Who-We-Are/General-Information/Foundation-Factsheet (last accessed 11 March 2015).

Randomized control trials: Abhijit Banerjee and Ester Duflo, *Poor Economics* (Public Affairs, 2011); and Martin Ravallion, 'Fighting Poverty One Experiment at a Time: Review of Poor Economics', *Journal of Economic Literature*, 50:1 (2012): 103–14.

CHAPTER 6: SUSTAINABLE DEVELOPMENT

Brundtland Commission: World Commission on the Environment and Development, *Our Common Future* (Oxford University Press, 1987).

Environmental degradation statistics: Conservation International's website, http://www.conservation.org/ (last accessed 11 March 2015); FAO 'Deforestation and Net Forest Area Change', http://www.fao.org/forestry/30515/en/ (last accessed 11 March 2015); FAO, 'Desertification Key Facts', http://www.ifad.org/english/desert/facts.htm (last accessed 11 March 2015); Deborah Sick, 'Environment and Development' in P. A. Haslam, J. Schafer, and P. Beaudet (eds), *Introduction to International Development: Approaches, Actors, and Issues* (Oxford University Press, 2012), pp. 313–32; UN, 'Water Scarcity', Water for Life Decade, http://www.un.org/waterforlifedecade/scarcity.shtml (last accessed 12 November 2015); UNICEF, *Progress on Sanitation and Drinking Water: MDG Assessment* (UNICEF and WHO, 2015), http://www.wssinfo.org/fileadmin/user_upload/resources/JMP-MDG-assessment-snapshot-in-English.pdf (last accessed 7 January 2016); and Gaia Vince, 'How the World's Oceans Could Be Running out of Fish', *BBC Smart Planet*, 21 September 2012, http://www.bbc.com/future/story/20120920-are-we-running- out-of-fish (last accessed 1 August 2015).

Club of Rome: Donella Meadows, Dennis Meadows, Jørgen Randers, and William Behrens, *The Limits to Growth: A Report for the Club of Rome's Project on the Predicament of Mankind* (Earth Island, 1972).

Climate change and mitigation of: Nicholas Stern, *Why Are We Waiting? The Logic, Urgency, and Promise of Tackling Climate Change* (MIT Press, 2015).

Planetary boundaries: Johan Rockström and Mattias Klum, *Big World, Small Planet: Abundance within Planetary Boundaries* (Bokförlaget Max Ström, 2015); and Global Footprint Network, www.footprintnetwork.org/ (last accessed 13 November 2015).

Environmental Kuznets Curve: Ian Goldin and Alan Winters, *The Economics of Sustainable Development* (Cambridge University Press, 1995).

Too many people? Ian Goldin (ed.), *Is the Planet Full?* (Oxford University Press, 2014).

Polluter pays principle and summits: Deborah Sick, 'Environment and Development' in P. A. Haslam, J. Schafer, and P. Beaudet (eds), *Introduction to International Development: Approaches, Actors, and Issues* (Oxford University Press, 2012), pp. 313–32.

Monetary value of the world's eco-system services: Robert Costanza, Ralph d'Arge, Rudolf de Groot, Stephen Farberk, Monica Grasso, Bruce Hannon, Karin Limburg, Shahid Naeem, Robert V. O'Neill, Jose Paruelo, Robert G. Raskin, Paul Sutton, and Marjan van den Belt, 'The Value of the World's Ecosystem Services and Natural Capital', *Nature*, 387 (15 May 1997): 253–60.

Future generations: Commission for Future Generations, *Now for the Long Term: The Report of the Oxford Martin Commission for Future Generations* (Oxford Martin School, University of Oxford, 2013).

Nordhaus's criticism of environmental discount rates: William Nordhaus, 'A Review of the *Stern Review on the Economics of Climate Change*', *Journal of Economic Literature*, XLV (2007): 686–702.

COP21: See the COP21 website, http://www.cop21paris.org/ (last accessed 12 November 2015).

CHAPTER 7: GLOBALIZATION AND DEVELOPMENT

Global flows and integration: Ian Goldin and Kenneth Reinert, *Globalization for Development: Meeting New Challenges* (Oxford University Press, 2012).

Commercial bank lending (15 largest emerging market economies): James Kynge, 'Emerging Market Capital Outflows Eclipse Financial Crisis Levels', *Financial Times*, 7 May 2015, http://www.ft.com/cms/s/0/cd212164-f429-11e4-bd16-00144feab7de.html#axzz3hgJPXV2J (Last accessed 23 September 2015); and Jonathan Wheatley and Sam Fleming, 'Capital Flight Darkens Economic Prospects for Emerging Markets', *Financial Times* (1 October 2015).

United States debt: US Treasury, *Debt Position and Activity Report* (June 2015), http://www.treasurydirect.gov/govt/reports/pd/pd_debtposactrpt_0615.pdf (last accessed 23 September 2015); and Ian Talley, 'U.S. Debt Held by Foreigners Hits Record $6.07 Trillion', *The Wall Street Journal* (17 October 2015), http://blogs.wsj.com/economics/2014/10/17/u-s-debt-held-by-foreigners-hits-record-6-07-trillion/ (last accessed 7 October 2015).

Developing countries and sovereign bonds: Elaine Moore and Jonathan Wheately, 'Emerging Market Bond Sell-off Gathers Pace', *Financial Times*, 9 June 2015, http://www.ft.com/cms/s/0/980afb1a-0dd0-11e5-9a65-00144feabdc0.html#axzz3hgJPXV2J (last accessed 23 September 2015).

Corporate bond issuance: Institute of International Finance, 'Corporate Debt in Emerging Markets: What Should We Be Worried about?' 15 March 2015, https://www.iif.com/publication/html-publication/corporate-debt-emerging-markets-what-should-we-be-worried-about (last accessed 23 September 2015); and John Schults, *Debt Capital Markets Review: Managing Underwriters: Full Year 2014* (Thomson Reuters, 2015), http://dmi.thomsonreuters.com/Content/Files/4Q2014_Global_Debt_Capital_Markets_Review.pdf (last accessed 23 September 2015).

Private equity flows: Bain & Company, *Global Private Equity Report 2015* (Bain and Company, Inc), http://www.bain.com/bainweb/PDFs/Bain_and_Company_Global_Private_Equity_Report_2015.pdf (last accessed 23 September 2015).

Private equity flows to Africa: EY, *Private Equity Round Up Africa* (EYGM Limited, 2014), http://www.ey.com/Publication/vwLUAssets/EY_-_Private_equity_roundup_-_Africa/$FILE/PE%20roundup%20Africa%202014_FR0117.pdf (last accessed 23 September 2015); and author's estimate of cumulative investment over the last two decades based on discussions with investors and the CDC.

Agricultural protectionism estimates: Author's calculations based on statistics from *OECD. Stat*, http://stats.oecd.org/ (last accessed 7 October 2015).

Cost of agricultural protectionism for consumers in the European Union and United States: Author's estimate based on Ian Goldin and Kenneth Reinert, *Globalization for Development: Trade, Finance, Aid, Migration and Policy*, revised edition (Palgrave, 2007), p. 64; and http://stats.oecd.org/ (last accessed 7 October 2015).

Potential gains in global income from Doha trade negotiations: David Laborde, Will Martin, and Dominique van der Mensbrugghe, 'Implications of the Doha Market Access Proposals for Developing Countries', *World Trade Review*, 11 (1) (2014): 1–25.

Benefits of agricultural protection for farmers: Author's estimate based on http://stats.oecd.org/, http://ec.europa.eu/eurostat, and http://www.usda.gov/ (last accessed 12 November 2015).

HIV/AIDS patents and Brazil, India, and South Africa: Jacqui Wise, 'Access to AIDS Medicine Stumbles on Trade Rules', *Bulletin of the World Health Organization*, 84 (5) (2006): 342–4.

Average health expenditure in the United States and sub-Saharan Africa: These figures relate to 2013 and are taken from World Bank, *World Development Indicators*, http://data.worldbank.org/ (last accessed 7 October 2015).

Measles initiative: The Measles and Rubella Initiative, 'Learn: The Problem' and 'Learn: The Solution' (American Red Cross, 2015), http://www.measlesrubellainitiative.org/ (last accessed, 7 October 2015).

Global biotechnology market and patents: Debra Strauss, 'The Application of TRIPS to GMOs: International Intellectual Property Rights and Biotechnology', *Stanford Journal of International Law*, 45 (2009): 287–320.

Technology and development: World Bank, *World Development Report 2016: Internet for Development* (World Bank, 2015); World Bank, 'Mobile Phone Payments Go Viral: M-PESA in Kenya', http://go.worldbank.org/XSGEPAIMO0 (last accessed 7 October 2015); E. F. Schumacher, *Small Is Beautiful: A Study of Economics as if People Mattered* (Blond and Briggs, 1973); and for a more detailed discussion of many of these issues see Ian Goldin and Kenneth Reinert, *Globalization for Development: Meeting New Challenges* (Oxford University Press, 2012), esp. pp. 228–36.

Scientific invention: see http://www.oxfordmartin.ox.ac.uk/research/programmes/ (last accessed 13 November 2015) for examples of scientific innovation.

Tax avoidance, transfer pricing, and underpaid tax bills: *The Economist* (2014), 'Corporate Tax Dodging: Transfer Policing' (20 September); BBC (2012), 'Apple Paid only 2% Corporation Tax outside US' (4 November), http://www.bbc.co.uk/news/business-20197710 (last accessed 23 September 2015); and Ian Goldin and Mike Mariathasan, *The Butterfly Defect: How Globalization Creates Systemic Risk, and What to Do about It* (Princeton University Press, 2014), p. 281.

Illicit commerce and slavery estimates: Moisés Naím, *Illicit* (Arrow, 2007); David A. Clark (ed.), *Adaptation, Poverty and Development: The Dynamics of Subjective Well-Being* (Palgrave, 2012), p. 79; and Larry Elliot, 'Modern Slavery Affects more than 35 Million People, Report Finds', *The Guardian* online (17 November 2014) http://www.theguardian.com/world/2014/nov/17/modern-slavery-

35-million-people-walk-free-foundation-report (last accessed 27 March 2015).

International migration: Ian Goldin, Geoffrey Cameron, and Meera Balarajan, *Exceptional People: How Migration Shaped our World and Will Define our Future* (Princeton University Press, 2012).

Number of international migrants: UNHCR, 'UNHCR report confirms worldwide rise in forced displacement in first half of 2015', Press Release (United Nations Refugee Agency, 18 December 2015); World Bank, 'Migration and Remittances: Recent Developments and Outlook', *Migration and Development Brief 24* (13 April 2015), p.4, http://siteresources.worldbank.org/INTPROSPECTS/Resources/334934-1288990760745/MigrationandDevelopmentBrief24.pdf (last accessed 30 September 2015), p. 1; and author's calculation using the data for 2013 from the above source for the estimates of migration between different regions.

Migrant remittances: Ian Goldin and Kenneth Reinert, *Globalization for Development: Meeting New Challenges* (Oxford University Press, 2012), p. 196; and World Bank, 'Migration and Remittances: Recent Developments and Outlook', *Migration and Development Brief 24* (13 April 2015), p. 4, http://siteresources.worldbank.org/INTPROSPECTS/Resources/334934-1288990760745/MigrationandDevelopmentBrief24.pdf (last accessed 30 September 2015), p. 5.

Impact of opening borders on growth: World Bank, *Global Economic Prospects: The Economics Implications of Remittances and Migration* (World Bank, 2005); and Kym Anderson and Bjørn Lomberg, 'Free Trade, Free Labour, Free Growth', Project Syndicate (2008), http://www.project-syndicate.org/commentary/free-trade–free-labor–free-growth (last accessed 2 August 2015).

Refugee statistics and number of forcibly displaced people: UNHCR, *Facts and Figures about Refugees* (2015), http://www.unhcr.org.uk/about-us/key-facts-and-figures.html (last accessed 2 August 2015); and Reuters in Berlin, 'Germany Raises Estimate on Refugee Arrivals to 800,000 This Year', *The Guardian* online (20 September

2015), http://www.theguardian.com/world/2015/aug/20/germany-raises-estimate-refugee-arrivals-800000 (last accessed 7 October 2015).

CHAPTER 8: THE FUTURE OF DEVELOPMENT

Global poverty reduction: *PovcalNet: The Online Tool For Poverty Measurement* (Development Research Group, World Bank), http://iresearch.worldbank.org/PovcalNet/index.htm?1 (last accessed 18 October 2015); and Marcio Cruz, James Foster, Bryce Quillin, and Philip Schellekens, 'Ending Extreme Poverty and Sharing Prosperity: Progress and Policies', *Policy Research Note* (World Bank, 2015).

International migration: Ian Goldin and Geoffrey Cameron, 'Migration Is Essential for Growth', *The European Financial Review* (20 December, 2011).

Our common future: Garrett Hardin, 'The Tragedy of the Commons', *Science,* 162 (1968): 1243–8; and Elinor Ostrom *Governing the Commons: The Evolution of Institutions for Collective Action* (Cambridge University Press, 1990).

Make poverty history: David Hulme, *Global Poverty: Global Governance and Poor People in the post-2015 Era,* second edition (Routledge, 2015); and Jeffrey Sachs, *The End of Poverty: How We Can Make it Happen in our Lifetime* (Penguin, 2005).

FURTHER READING

CHAPTER 1: WHAT IS DEVELOPMENT?

David A. Clark, *Visions of Development: A Study of Human Values* (Edward Elgar, 2002), esp. chapter 1.

David A. Clark, 'Capability Approach' in D. A. Clark (ed.), *The Elgar Companion to Development Studies* (Edward Elgar, 2006), pp. 32–45.

Michael Cowen and Robert Shenton, *Doctrines of Development* (Routledge, 2008).

Ian Goldin and Ken Reinert, *Globalization for Development: Meeting New Challenges* (Oxford University Press, 2012).

Norman Hicks and Paul Streeten, 'Indicators of Development: The Search for a Basic Needs Yardstick', *World Development*, 7 (1979): 567–80.

Edmund Phelps, *Mass Flourishing: How Grassroots Innovation Created Jobs, Challenge, and Change* (Princeton University Press, 2014).

Wolfgang Sachs, *The Development Dictionary: A Guide to Knowledge as Power* (Zed Books, 1992).

Frances Stewart, 'Basic Needs, Capabilities, and Human Development', in A. Offer (ed.), *In Pursuit of the Quality of Life* (Oxford University Press, 1996), pp. 46–65.

Joseph Stiglitz, Amartya K. Sen, and Jean-Paul Fitoussi, *Mismeasuring our Lives: Why GDP Doesn't Add Up* (New Press, 2010).

UNDP, *Human Development Report* (Oxford University Press, 1990).

CHAPTER 2: HOW DOES DEVELOPMENT HAPPEN?

Irma Adelman and Cynthia Morris, 'Development History and its Implications for Development Theory', *World Development*, 25 (6) (1997): 831–40.

Ronald Ayres (ed.), *Development Studies: A Reader* (University of Greenwich Press, 1998), esp. part II on 'theories of development'.

Bruce Herrick and Charles Kindleberger, *Economic Development*, fourth edition (McGraw-Hill, 1983).

Gerald Meier (ed.), *Leading Issues in Development Economics*, sixth edition (Oxford University Press, 1995), esp. extracts on 'Historical Perspectives', 'Lewis's Dual-Sector Model', 'Linkage Effects and Industrialization—Hirschman', 'Trade as an "Engine of Growth"', 'Market Forces and Development', 'Government Intervention', and 'Rent Seeking and DUP Activities'.

Gerald Meier and James Rauch, *Leading Issues in Development Economics*, Eighth edition (Oxford University Press, 2005)—Chapters on 'The (Proper) Role of the State in

Less Developed Countries', and 'Rent Seeking and Government Failure'.

Douglas North, *Institutions, Institutional Change and Economic Performance* (Cambridge University Press, 1990).

Narcís Serra and Joseph Stiglitz (eds), *The Washington Consensus Reconsidered: Towards A New Global Governance* (Oxford University Press, 2008).

John Toye and Richard Toye, 'The Origins and Interpretation of the Prebisch-Singer Thesis', *History of Political Economy*, 35 (3) (2003): 437–67.

Andrew Webster, *Introduction to the Sociology of Development* (Macmillan, 1990), chapter 3 on modernization theory.

John Williamson, 'What Washington Means by Policy Reform', in J. Williamson (ed.), *Latin American Adjustment: How Much Has Happened* (Institute for International Economics, 1990), pp. 7–38.

CHAPTER 3: WHY ARE SOME COUNTRIES RICH AND OTHERS POOR?

Anthony Atkinson, *Inequality: What Can Be Done?* (Harvard University Press, 2015).

Ha-Joon Chang, *Kicking Away the Ladder: Development Strategy in Historical Perspective* (Anthem, 2002).

Sharad Chari and Stuart Corbridge (eds), *The Development Reader* (Routledge, 2006), Part 1 on factors underlying growth differentials.

Paul Collier, *The Bottom Billion: Why the Poorest Countries Are Failing and What Can Be Done about It* (Oxford University Press, 2007).

Christopher Cramer, *Civil War Is Not a Stupid Thing: Accounting for Violence in Developing Countries* (Hurst, 2006).

Debraj Ray, *Development Economics* (Princeton University Press, 1998), esp. pp. 74–84 on 'convergence' and pp. 199–209 on Kuznet's 'inverted-U hypothesis'.

Dani Rodrik, Arvind Subramanian, and Francesco Trebbi, 'Institutions Rule: The Primacy of Institutions over Integration and Geography in Economic Development', *Journal of Economic Growth*, 9 (2) (2004): 131–65.

Jeffrey Sachs, Andre Mellinger, and John Gallup, 'The Geography of Poverty and Wealth', *Scientific American*, 284 (2001): 70–6, on the 'bad' geography thesis.

James Scott, *Seeing like a State: How Certain Schemes to Improve the Human Condition Have Failed* (Yale University Press, 1998).

Amartya K. Sen, *Development as Freedom* (Oxford University Press, 1999).

CHAPTER 4: WHAT CAN BE DONE TO ACCELERATE DEVELOPMENT?

Basil Davidson, *The Black Man's Burden: Africa and the Curse of the Nation-state* (Currey, 1992).

Jean Dréze and Amartya K. Sen, *An Uncertain Glory: India and Its Contradictions* (Princeton University Press, 2013).

Shailaja Fennell and Madeleine Arnot (eds), *Gender Education and Equality in a Global Context: Conceptual Frameworks and Policy Perspectives* (Routledge, 2009).

Naila Kabeer, *Reversed Realities: Gender Hierarchies in Development* (Verso, 1995).

World Bank, *World Development Report 2011: Conflict, Security, and Development* (World Bank, 2011).

CHAPTER 5: THE EVOLUTION OF DEVELOPMENT AID

Frik De Beer and Hennie Swanepoel, *Introduction to Development Studies*, second edition (Oxford University Press, 2000), Unit 15 on aid and debt.

Global Development Incubator, *Innovative Financing for Development* (Dalberg, 2014), http://www.globaldevincubator. org/wp-content/uploads/2014/09/Innovative-Financing-for-Development.pdf (last accessed 1 October 2015).

Giles Carbonnier, *Humanitarian Economics: War, Disaster and the Global Aid Market* (C Hurst and Co, 2015).

Ian Goldin, Halsey Rogers, and Nicholas Stern, 'The Role and Effectiveness of Development Assistance: Lessons from World Bank Experience', in *A Case Study for Aid: Building a Consensus for Development Experience* (World Bank, 2002): 125–83.

David Hulme, 'The Millennium Development Goals (MDGs): A Short History of the World's Biggest Promise', BWPI Working Paper 100 (Brooks World Poverty Institute, 2009).

CHAPTER 6: SUSTAINABLE DEVELOPMENT

Commission for Future Generations, *Now for the Long Term: The Report of the Oxford Martin Commission for Future*

Generations (Oxford Martin School, University of Oxford, 2013).

Ian Goldin and Alan Winters (eds.), *The Economics of Sustainable Development* (Cambridge University Press, 1995).

Deborah Sick, 'Environment and Development' in P. A. Haslam, J. Schafer, and P. Beaudet (eds), *Introduction to International Development: Approaches, Actors, and Issues* (Oxford University Press, 2012), pp. 313–32.

Nicholas Stern, *Why Are We Waiting: The Logic, Urgency, and Promise of Tackling Climate Change* (MIT Press, 2015).

CHAPTER 7: GLOBALIZATION AND DEVELOPMENT

Ian Goldin, *Divided Nations: Why Global Governance Is Failing and What We Can Do about It* (Oxford University Press, 2013).

Ian Goldin, Geoffrey Cameron, and Meera Balarajan, *Exceptional People: How Migration Shaped our World and Will Define our Future* (Princeton University Press, 2011).

Ian Goldin and Mike Mariathasan, *The Butterfly Defect: How Globalization Creates Systemic Risks, and What to Do about It* (Princeton University Press, 2014).

Ian Goldin and Kenneth Reinert, *Globalization for Development: Meeting New Challenges* (Oxford University Press, 2012), chapters 3, 4, 6, and 7 on finance, trade, migration, and ideas.

Ankie Hoogvelt, *Globalisation and the Post-Colonial World: The New Political Economy of Development* (Palgrave Macmillan, 1997).

CHAPTER 8: THE FUTURE OF DEVELOPMENT

Angus Deaton, *The Great Escape: Health, Wealth, and the Origins of Inequality* (Princeton University Press, 2013).

Ian Goldin (ed.), *Is the Planet Full?* (Oxford University Press, 2014).

David Hulme, *Global Poverty: Global Governance and Poor People in the post-2015 Era,* second edition (Routledge, 2015).

Jeffrey Sachs, *The End of Poverty: How We Can Make it Happen in our Lifetime* (Penguin, 2005).

UN, *Millennium Development Goals Report 2015* (United Nations, 2015).

INDEX

Boxes, figures and tables are indicated by an italic *b*, *f* or *t* following the page number.

Index

Index